# CONTENTS

# BAE OR NAH

## FINDING THE LOVE OF YOUR LIFE

# INTRODUCTION:

Bae – an acronym that stands for "before anyone else," or shortened version of baby or babe, another word for sweetie. Urban Dictionary

Most people want a Bae. You're probably reading this because you want a Bae. In fact, you don't just want Bae to be your girlfriend or your boyfriend. Eventually, you want to marry Bae. You want to find the person of your dreams and live happily ever after with them.

Of course, finding *that* Bae is easier said than done. It's not as easy as it looks in the movies. It's not that we don't have an abundance of tools to help us. In fact, we have more than any generation before us. We have Apps, Social Media, Websites, Dating Programs, Books and more available to help us find the one for us. Yet, for many, it's not enough.

You see, God has a Bae in mind for you. Someone that is perfect for you and the life that he wants you to live. You can't find *that Bae* without his help. You can't identify *that Bae* without having the spiritual tools that God provides.

The truth is that you need help from Heaven to navigate this season of life. You need help from Heaven in determining the right criteria to use in evaluating whether or not to enter or stay in a relationship with someone that you may have a shared attraction with. You need help from heaven to properly determine if the one that you're attracted to, thinking about, talking to or dating right now is God's Bae for you.

That's why I've written this book. I believe God is eager to help you and that he wants to use me to do it! I believe that, with his help, you can actually find & identify the one he has for you. I believe that he's already written your love story & that, as you follow the teachings in this book, you will actually live it!

So if you're young & single or newly single, open your heart and mind to what God has to say to you through the Bible. Your life will never be the same again. In fact, I'm looking forward to reading your love story one day. I'm that confident that this book will prepare you for, & ultimately, lead you to Bae! Are you ready? Let's get it...

# CHAPTER 1: GOD HAS SOMEONE IN MIND FOR YOU

T he process to finding God's Bae for you is different. It's not just a natural process. That's how we normally think about relationships. A guy likes a girl who likes him back. They eventually date, get married and, somehow, live happily ever after. And sure, that's the basics, but when we're talking about God's Bae for you, that person that is perfect for you & the future that God has for you, well, that process is Supernatural. You need God's help for that to happen.

So let's look at the very first couple and how God brought them together. There are some principles in this story that will reveal how God has wanted to work all along.

> Then the LORD God said, "It is not good for the man to be alone. I will make a helper who is just right for him." Genesis 2:18, 21-24 NLT

If you were to back up a few scriptures, you would find out that God creates the man and places him in the Garden of Eden. So the man has a home. God then gives the man a job. And, of course, there's food in the Garden. I want you to notice that the man had a home, had a job and food before God brought him a woman. If a man doesn't have those 3 things, he's not ready for marriage!

God also gave the man instructions to not eat of the fruit that was on the Tree of the Knowledge of Good and Evil. Apparently the man obeyed that instruction up until this point. He demonstrated that he had a willingness to obey God, & the discipline to do it, before God brought a woman into his life.

Clearly, a man needs to actually be following God before he's qualified for God to bring a woman of God into his life. If he's not ready to follow God until he's met a woman, if he's just following God because of that woman, well, something is already off. He's not ready for God's Bae for him.

I can imagine a woman reading this and thinking "Pastor Dre! You just wiped out 95% of the men in the country in the opening chapter!" That's alright. You only need one.

> So the LORD God caused the man to fall into a deep sleep. While the man slept, the LORD God took out one of the man's ribs and closed up the opening. Then the LORD God made a woman from the rib... Genesis 2:21, 22

This is deep. God literally did surgery on this man. And he literally took a rib out of the man's body. Then, God made a woman from the rib! This is the only part of God's new creation that he formed in this way.

Everything else was created out of the dust of the ground but when it came to the woman, God chose to create her out of the man. There's some significance to that. In fact, later in the Bible, God constantly reminds us that she is a part of him. He says to married men that she is a part of his body, that loving her is loving himself.

...and he brought her to the man. "At last!" the man exclaimed. "This one is bone from my bone, and flesh from my flesh! She will be called 'woman,' because she was taken from 'man.'" This explains why a man leaves his father and mother and is joined to his wife, and the two are united into one. Genesis 2:22-24 NLT

Here is the very first wedding ceremony! God walked her down the aisle!

God had this written for us because he wanted it to serve as an example for us. In this story is a pattern that God wanted men and women to follow from here on out. A man leaves his father and his mother and he cleaves unto his woman (the word 'wife' here comes from a Hebrew word that means woman).

Marriage was God's idea. God literally invented marriage. And for most people, God's will is that they be married. If that desire is in your heart, to be married one day, I want you to know that God wants it for you too. He wants to give you the desires of your heart.

Take delight in the LORD, and he will give you your heart's desires. Psalm 37:4 NLT

In Psalms 126, the Bible talks about God finally giving his people their hearts desire to go home to Jerusalem. It says that for them it was like they were dreaming. It shared that they were laughing and singing because of what God had done. God wants to meet this desire for you as well. He cares about the details of your life. And if you want Bae, he wants to bring them to you!

I know what I'm doing. I have it all planned out - plans to take care of you, not abandon you, plans to give you the future you hope for. Jeremiah 29:11

In fact, God has already written your love story. I'm gonna say it again because it was good. God has already written your love story. He sees the end from the beginning, right? He already has it planned out! He's going to give you the future that you long for! God is a phenomenal Matchmaker!

> The Lord will work out his plans for my life - for your faithful love, O Lord, endures forever. Don't abandon me, for you made me. Psalm 138:8 NLT

God's actually focused on working out this plan that he has for you. He's focused on helping you live out the story that he's written for you and your Bae. He's actually working on it right now.

I was having a conversation with someone the other day that is happily married. She was marveling about the fact that when she was longing to be married, the man that she is now married too (who lived thousands of miles away) was actually breathing and living his life. She had no idea who God had in mind for her, but all along, God was preparing him for her.

As you're reading this book, you may be thinking the same thing. "Hey, I want to be married one day." And I want you to know that you may know Bae yet but God does. You may not know them yet but God knows them. You may not know where Bae is but God does. God knows when you're going to meet. God knows how your relationship will flow. God has already planned all of this!

That's something you can rest in as you wait to meet Bae.
Now, some people struggle with the idea of God having someone, in particular, in mind for you so let's look at what I like to call a 'Matchmaking Chapter' in the Bible. This entire chapter is about God finding a wife for his servant, Isaac.

**God The MatchMaker**

> Abraham was now a very old man, and the LORD had blessed him in every way. One day Abraham said to his oldest servant, the man in charge of his household, "Take an oath by putting your hand under my thigh. Swear by the LORD, the God of heaven and earth, that you will not allow my son to marry one of these local Canaanite women. Go instead to my homeland, to my relatives, and find a wife there for my son Isaac." Genesis 24:1-3 NLT

Abraham had his servant swear by the Lord because this was very, very important. He couldn't get this wrong. It was very important because Isaac was a covenant man. God had a covenant to bring through him, the nation of Israel, and ultimately, Jesus. So this woman is very important. He *had* to get it right.

And do you know what? You have to get this right too. Choosing who you marry may be the most important decision you will ever make in your life (outside of the decision to follow Jesus).

> The servant asked, "But what if I can't find a young woman who is willing to travel so far from home? Should I then take Isaac there to live among your relatives in the land you came from?" "No!" Abraham responded. "Be careful never to take my son there. For the LORD, the God of heaven, who took me from my father's house and my native land, solemnly promised to give this land to my descendants. He will send his angel ahead of you, and he will see to it that you find a wife there for my son. If she is unwilling to come back with you, then you are free from this oath of mine. But under no circumstances are you to take my son there." So the servant took an oath by putting his hand under the thigh of his master, Abraham. He swore to follow Abraham's instructions. Genesis 24:4-6 NLT

Aren't you glad our parents don't get to choose our Bae! Whew! I can just imagine who mine would have picked!

Anyway, Abraham had a very specific criteria he wanted his servant to use in choosing a wife for Isaac. Frankly, finding what he was looking for was going to be very difficult. It would be like finding a needle in a haystack to just to go to this city and happen to find somebody that is related to Abraham, who by the way is beautiful and single and would be willing to leave her home including everyone and everything that she has ever known, to go marry a man she had not even met, and live in a situation that she has never even experienced. I mean, she's literally going to have to just walk into the unknown. This seems like an impossible ask.

You may feel that way about dating right now, especially if you're a female. You may feel like there's no real, godly men out here. You may feel like there's no one that would want me. If you're a man of God you also may feel like there's no real women of God available. The good news is 'with God nothing is impossible!' Notice, once again, what Abraham said about the role God would play in this.

> For the LORD, the God of heaven, who took me from my father's house and my native land, solemnly promised to give this land to my descendants. He will send his angel ahead of you, and he will see to it that you find a wife there for my son. Genesis 24:5 NLT

Abraham is saying that God is going to send an Angel, a match-making Angel, to help! This isn't Cupid. This is *better* than Cupid! This is the real match-making Angel and this Angel is going to make sure that they find Isaac's wife. This is supernatural!

Abraham believed that the same God that brought him out of his family's house, the same God that brought him out of his country, the same God that told him that he's given him this land, the same God that had been taking care of him and had blessed him in every area of his life, was going to make this happen too.

If you're a Christian, God's has probably already done some supernatural things for you. He saved you. He comforted you. He healed you. He sent somebody to you to help you to know about Jesus. He gave you a new job. He brought you to your church. He brought money when you needed it. He did supernatural things in those areas of your life. He will do a work in this area of Your life as well! This is supernatural!

> Then he loaded ten of Abraham's camels with all kinds of expensive gifts from his master, and he traveled to distant Aram-naharaim. There he went to the town where Abraham's brother Nahor had settled. He made the camels kneel beside a well just outside the town. It was evening, and the women were coming out to draw water. "O LORD, God of my master, Abraham," he prayed. "Please give me success today, and show unfailing love to my master, Abraham. See, I am standing here beside this spring, and the young women of the town are coming out to draw water. Genesis 24:10-12 NLT

Something worth noting, is that he didn't need 10 camels to travel. He needed 10 camels so she could know that Abraham's son, Isaac, had money. Money matters to women just like looks matter to men!

Notice that he goes where the available young women usually are. Man of God, if you want a godly woman, you got to go where to godly women are. Right? You're not going to find her at the club right now. If she's still at the club she's not ready for you.

> "O LORD, God of my master, Abraham," he prayed. "Please give me success today, and show unfailing love to my

master, Abraham. See, I am standing here beside this spring, and the young women of the town are coming out to draw water. This is my request. I will ask one of them 'Please give me a drink from your jug.' And if she says, 'Yes, have a drink, and I will water your camels too!'- let her be the one you have selected as Isaac's wife. This I how I will know that you have shown unfailing love to my master." Genesis 24:12-14 NLT

This is supernatural and Abraham's servant understands that. He realizes that he's going to need God's help so what does he do? He prays. In his prayer he puts out what Christians commonly call a 'fleece.' In other words, "God if you do this then I know its you."

If you're a Christian, you don't have to do that anymore. God has literally put himself on the inside of your heart and he will guide you from the inside out. But notice what he's trying to accomplish here. He believes God has somebody in mind for Isaac. He believed that God was looking at the earth and saying "I've got somebody that is best for Isaac."

He believed what Abraham had said, that God would send his angel to that individual and work to help him meet her. And he was right! God did have someone in mind for Isaac. Her name was Rebekah!

Before he had finished praying, he saw a young woman named Rebekah coming out with her water jug on her shoulder. She was the daughter of Bethuel, who was the sone of Abraham's brother Nahor and his wife, Milcah. Rebekah was very beautiful and old enough to be married, but she was still a virgin. She went down to the spring, filled her jug, and came up again. Genesis 24:15, 16 NLT

Just like God had someone in mind for Isaac. God has someone in mind for you!

I know this isn't necessarily a universal view among Christians. There are times when you hear good meaning people preach differently than this. But I have a real problem with that preaching because we seem to believe that there is a perfect will of God for everything in our lives, except for this. There's a perfect will of God for the church you're supposed to be at. There's a perfect will of God for the calling you're supposed to be pursuing There's a perfect will of God for the city that you're supposed to be in. There's a perfect will of God for the job that you're supposed to have. But when it comes to the most important decision that you'll have on his earth outside of following Jesus, well, that's entirely that's up to you. That's just not biblical.

The truth of the matter is that you don't get to determine who is God's perfect will for your spouse. No more than you get to choose your pastor. No more than you get to choose what you're called to do. Now you can choose to go against God's plan. But if you want God's best, God has someone in mind.

"Well, pastor," you may say, "People have free will. In this story they mentioned that its possible that she not be willing to come." Yeah, that's true. That's absolutely true. God can have somebody in mind for you. And you could be the person that he has a mind for them and they could choose to say no. People do it before they get married. Some people even do it *after* they marry. They just decide to backslide and say "I don't want God's plan for my life anymore."

Do you think that surprises God? Do you think he says "Oops, I didn't plan for that." When you're on a road trip in your car and are using Siri or some other GPS device to get to your destination, let's just say that you're trying to drive to Texas from Michigan, if you make a wrong turn what does Siri do? She gives you a new route to get to the same destination.

Well, God has all of this figured out. So if somebody decides to not choose God's Bae for them, God is not surprised. He saw this coming and he has someone else in mind who will fit just fine (and get their benefits!). For all we know, that someone may have had the person God had planned for them make the same decision.

My point is that God still has someone in mind for you! And you want God's best for you. You don't want your choice. You don't want Ishmael. You want Isaac.

Remember when God told Abraham that he was going to bring a great nation out of him. After 13 years of waiting, Abraham and Sarah decided that God's way wasn't working. They took Sarah's servant, Hagar, and gave her to Abraham to have children with. Abraham and Hagar then had a baby named Ishmael. And even though God loved Ishmael, he wasn't God's choice to be the heir that God used to create the nation of Israel through.

Having Ishmael created problems. Big problems. Too many people are dating their 'Ishmael's' right now because they're just tired and fed up with waiting. They're saying "I want to get married. My biological clock is ticking. I've just got to go find somebody." And that's just not what you want. You would rather stay alone than be with the person that God did not choose for you to be with. It is better to be lonely alone than to be lonely in a marriage.

God has someone in mind for you and you want God's best. And when God brings them, don't you dare tell God 'No.' As human beings, we have a tendency to nitpick things and you can nitpick your way right out of Bae! At some point you have to get past even some of our physical preferences (which *are* important - We'll talk about that) and start paying attention to what is God saying as well as to the character of the individual we're considering because that's what's really going to matter.

There is such a thing as God's best person for you, the perfect will of God for your life in this area and that is the person you want. *God's* Bae for you. And God has actually made it possible for you to know whether or not a person is his choice for you!

# CHAPTER 2: GOD'S STANDARDS FOR BAE

This is my request. I will ask one of them 'Please give me a drink from your jug.' And if she says, 'Yes, have a drink, and I will water your camels too!'- let her be the one you have selected as Isaac's wife. This I how I will know that you have shown unfailing love to my master." Genesis 24:14 NLT

T he process of discovering the person that God has in mind for you requires being able to define what you're looking for. Once you know what you're looking for, you must evaluate your options by those standards.

For example, if you were on a dating app like Tinder or Bumble, you open the app already having an idea of what you're attracted to physically. What happens when you see someone who doesn't match that standard, you swipe left. If you see someone that does, you swipe right.

You know what you're looking for and if someone doesn't meet your standards you decide to not waste your or their time. If they do meet your standards then you hope to investigate whether or not there is an attraction there that is more than physical.

There are standards that we ought to have when it comes to dating, when it comes to considering marrying someone. We really should stick by those standards because those standards are tools to help you to know whether or not this is God's Bae for you.

> Prove all things. Hold fast that which is good.

> 1 Thessalonians 5:21 KJV

That's one of the things that we can get from this scripture. When examining whether or not something is from God or not, we should test it. If you're considering or are presently dating someone, then put the relationship to the test. Ask yourself "What are my standards? Do they meet these standards? Is this Bozo or Boaz?"

In the Bible, there's a love story between Ruth and Boaz, a kind & wealthy man. God brought them together just like he did Isaac and Rebekah. Sometimes you're trying to find *Boaz* and here's *Bozo*! If you're not careful, you fall for Bozo (or Delilah instead of Rebekah!) because you don't evaluate them early according to your standards.

To help you with this I'm going to give you some questions to ask yourself when determining if this may be Bae or Nah:

## Question #1: Are you attracted to them?

> Rebekah was very beautiful and old enough to be married, but she was still a virgin. She went down to the spring, filled her jug, and came up again. Genesis 24:15, 16 NLT

This one is obvious but I still want to talk about it. If you look at the book of Esther and you read about Esther's love story, you will find that they had women go through a year's worth of beauty treatments before they even brought them before the King! Not to say that we should do that, but I do think that we need to acknowledge that beauty matters, that attraction matters.

Now, let me say that I understand that the word attraction means different things to different people. I remember doing a message along these lines and I was talking about attraction and some women jumped on me because they thought I was saying that he had to be cute. They made sure I understand that some of them didn't care if he was cute. Some of them even said they don't like cute guys! They said they want to be the cute one in the relationship! Lol! Well, I get it. I'm not saying he has to look a certain way. I'm saying you need to be attracted to him although that attraction may not have much to do with how he looks. For guys though, looks are a huge part of attraction.

I heard this joke once about this pastor who wanted to get married. He happened to be a guest speaker at a church service and he heard a woman sing right before he was to speak. She had an angelic voice and she was very anointed. The power of God fell in the room when she sang. The man thought they'd be a great team because of how anointed she was & how great a singer she was. So sure enough, they started dating, got married and had the wedding night. The next morning, he rolled over and saw her without her makeup. He was shocked and horrified and he said "Sing, Baby! Sing!"

Spiritual attributes are important, but you need to be attracted to them. This is someone that you're supposed to have sex with consistently for the rest of your life. (Really two or three times a week is really ideal for most couples.) You really need to be attracted to them because that's a requirement. You should *want* to sleep with them. Not dread it. Women and men can be attracted to different things in a potential partner, but God's plan is that you be very attracted to Bae.

## Question #2: Are they a mature Christian?

Let's start with 'Are they a Christian?' If you are a Christian, it makes zero sense for you to date someone that is not. The Bible calls that being "unequally yoked" and it creates big problems not only in your relationship with them but in the raising of your future kids. But it's not good enough if they're a Christian. A lot of people say that they are a Christian but you'd never know it by how they live. The question that you need to ask yourself is are they a mature Christian?

The Bible says, "you will know them by their fruits," by how they behave. You don't know what people's character is by what they say, or even where they came from. You know it by how they act.

So once again, let's look at this again in Genesis 24. Remember what the servant asked? He asked that this woman would be the one that would not only give him water, but that she would voluntarily offer to give water to his camels.

> Running over to her, the servant said, "Please give me a little drink of water from your jug." "Yes, my lord," she answered, "have a drink." And she quickly lowered her jug from her shoulder and gave him a drink. When she had given him a drink, she said, "I'll draw water for your camels, too, until they have had enough to drink. So she quickly emptied her jug into the watering trough and ran back to the well to draw water for all his camels The servant watched her in silence, wondering whether or not the Lord had given him success in his mission.

> Genesis 24:17-21

He's a stranger! Although the culture was definitely different than today, this is still a stranger approaching her and asking for water and she gladly gave him some. She was sweet.

Nowadays, there seems to have been a premium placed on woman being tough or having attitudes. Some of the songs that we sing and some of the role models that we have seem to champion being sassy and difficult. However, that is not what a Man of God wants in a woman. He wants what we see here. Instead of being difficult, instead of looking to be served, she volunteered to serve. She didn't just offer him water but she looked over at his camels and realized that they were probably thirsty too and she volunteered to help them.

Think about it for a second. What woman is going to look at a man's camels and say, "I'm going to get water for your camels." Come on! Nowadays some would say "Yo camels stink! Why are you bringing them around here? How dare you bring them close to me?!"

I'm making it funny, but am I right? Guys don't want that. They might be friends with that. They might play with that but they don't want to marry that. They want a sweet woman.

You see, this is extraordinary kindness. I read an article a while ago and it was talking about the number one trait of couples that make it is kindness. They're just kind to each other. So even when they disagree with each other, even when they have an issue, they can still find a way to be kind while addressing it.

See, what you're trying to do is evaluate a potential Bae from the inside out, not the outside in. The fact is some people never grow up. And you can't just marry someone based on potential. You'd be in error thinking that one day they would grow into the person that you need.

You actually want somebody that's already grown, that already has good attributes. I like something that someone once said, "Don't marry a man, unless you would be proud to have a son exactly like him." Let's flip that on its head as well. "Don't marry a woman unless you'd be proud to have a daughter exactly like her." Someone else said "A man first must find himself before he is ready to find you."

A woman of substance shouldn't want a man that doesn't have strong character. This story is talking about her character because the story is about her but the principle applies to him as well. He needs to find himself. He needs to have matured before you even bother to start the process of dating him.

Part of the problem that we have today with this is this thinking that there's not enough good men out here so women better grab one when they can etc. That kind of thinking has caused women to be the ones to chase after these men. And it's caused them to take on boys instead of a men.

A number of years ago, I was privileged to be on a panel at the Essence Festival in Atlanta. I remember being in this room packed with young black women. I think I was the only guy up on the panel. The question that came up was "is it okay for a woman to pursue a man" and overwhelmingly the women on the stage said "yes!" So, you know, I had to say something. I told them "no." The Bible says, "he that findeth a wife", right? Not she that chases down, traps or handcuffs a husband. They just dismissed me because there's this desperation that has infected so many women. But let me tell you, a man likes to chase women, not for her to find him.

If as a woman, you are jumping in guys DMs and then wondering why you can't find God's Bae, its because he isn't looking for you to jump in his DMs, he looking to jump into yours.

Then at last, when the camels had finished drinking, he took

BAE OR NAH: FINDING THE LOVE OF YOUR LIFE

out a gold ring for our nose and two large gold bracelets for a wrist. "Whose daughter are you?" he asked. "And please tell me, would your father have any room to put us up for the night?" I am the daughter of Behuel," she replied. "My grandparents are Nahor and Milcah. Ye, we have plenty of straw and feed for the camels, and we have room for guests." The man bowed low and worshiped the Lord. "Praise the Lord, the God of my master, Abraham," he said. "The Lord has shown unfailing love and faithfulness to my master, for he has led me straight to my master's relatives." Genesis 24:22-27 NLT

Rebekah was beautiful, kind, and it seemed like God had led him to her. However, this servant still had a criteria that he had received from Abraham that she needed to meet before he could be sure this was a God-led endeavor. When he found out that this is actually the granddaughter of Abraham's brother he knew that the angel had done his work and God had brought them together.

This was him proving all things by evaluating her. That's a big part of what the dating process is all about. That's why the main activity you should do in dating is talking. I actually believe in this day and age, and this has happened more because of COVID, dating by Zoom, Skype or FaceTime is can actually be superior to dating in-person sometimes because you're required to talk. And I mean talk and talk and talk and talk and talk. So you get to actually interview the person, know the person and it saves you from doing other things you have no business doing until you're married!

# CHAPTER 3: MATURE OR NAH?

**W**ell, how do you know whether or not they're a mature Christian or not? Here's some attributes to look for:

**They Have Developed The Habits of a Christian**

What are those habits? Well, they have daily time with God in prayer and in the Bible. You need them to have this relationship with God so that when they can't hear you, they can hear him. When they don't feel like doing right by you, or doing right period, God can get their attention. When you end up with somebody that doesn't really have this relationship and they decide they are done with you, they can blow up your life!

This is also why, even when you are married, that you need to pray for Bae. Everyone has free will, so they can ultimately choose to do wrong no matter how much praying you do, but by praying regularly for them you give them the best opportunity to choose to do the right thing.

The best thing to do, however, is to find somebody that already has a true, living relationship with God. Someone that already praises him, reads their Bible, serves in their church, talks to people about Jesus, etc. That's a mature Christian.

**They have the Fruit of the Spirit in Their Life**

The fruit of the Spirit are found in Galatians chapter 5 and the very first one is Love. Love is self-less, right? You want the person that's self-less, not selfish, nor self-centered. Here's a good thing to check out... In your conversations with them are they constantly patting themselves on the back? How many times do they use the word I? If the answer is alot, I can guarantee you, that even if they get you, they aren't going to be thinking about what's best for you very much. They will be thinking about what's best for them.

You need a person that has already developed to a place where they actually think about others before they think about themselves. And you need to be developed in the same way. You need somebody who has a servant's heart, someone that is sweet or a gentlemen.

The rest of the fruit of the Spirit includes Joy, Peace, Goodness, Kindness, and Self-control. A mature Christian has Self-Control. If he or she is trying to sleep with you before they marry you they aren't for you. They don't have self control yet. That leads to the next point.

**They are Living Pure**
They're not having sex. They don't just stop because they met you. They're not watching porn. They don't have vices in their life. They don't drink. They don't smoke. They don't vape. They don't do drugs. They don't gamble. They don't cuss. Mature Christians don't cuss. They just don't. This even applies to some of the media that they may watch.

**They Know their God-given Assignment**

They know what God has placed them on the earth to do. Often, we Christians call this their 'calling.' They may not even be fully in that calling yet but they are on the way. They have a total dedication to God's plan for their life and God's way of doing things. We'll talk a little more about that one in a minute.

## They are a Good Steward over their Money, Body, & Home

You don't want someone who is undisciplined financially, because if that's the case, you're going to have to live with it. You don't want someone who is undisciplined in regards to their body, because once again, you're going to have to live with it. You don't want someone whose home is just a complete and total mess, because once again, you're going to have to live with that. You want someone that has Self-Control in these areas.

## Question #3: What does your Family and Friends Say?

It seems that everyone has family and friends that make them wonder if they're sane! And that every Christian has family and friends who may say they are a Christian but don't really live like one. Your focus, on this question of Bae or Nah, needs to shift to those that really do love God. It needs to shift to those that have a relationship with him and are committed to helping you recognize what God is saying to you. What do they have to say about your relationship?

In Genesis 24, Abraham's servant comes to Laban and Bethuel and asks them to tell him whether or not they were going to allow this to happen. He was looking for a Yes or No answer. (At some point, you do need to get to that point of a Yes or No). Laban and Bethel replied, *"The Lord has obviously brought you here. So there's nothing we can say. Here's Rebekah, take her and go, yes. Let her be the wife of your master's son."* Get this. *"As the Lord has directed."*

They recognized that God was in this. God has given you your family and friends as a safety net. This would include your spiritual family, your pastor or ministry team that you have at your church. Now, that doesn't mean they have final say over whether or not you should be with this person because sometimes even well-meaning people can give you wrong instruction, but it does mean their role is to help you to ascertain what God is saying.

The Bible says in Proverbs 24 *"For by wise counsel, you will wage your own war. And in a multitude of counselors, there is safety."* So its good to have multiple people in your life who will help you to realize what God is saying. And that's why you have to ask yourself the question. "What are my family and friends saying? What kind of counsel are they giving? Are they saying, This person is not for you or are they agreeing that this might be Bae?"

I watched this happen with my sister. Her husband is from England. They met online on a Christian dating site. At first glance, this didn't look like it could lead to anything. He was in England and there were other factors. But over time it began to appear to be supernatural. I and another Pastor friend were instrumental in helping her to not dismiss the relationship and now years later, they are happily married with a miracle baby. God uses the people in our lives more than we know. You need to fully include them in the evaluation process.

## Question#4: Do your Assignments Match?

In Genesis 24, there was a little dispute when the time came for her to actually leave. Although her family had approved of this major life change. They didn't want her to leave right away. And so in verse 38 they call Rebecca and ask her, "are you willing to go with this man"? And she replied, "yes, I will go." And here's the thing. She was doing something that was wild. Right? Leaving everybody, leaving everything. She did the same thing that Abraham did in Genesis 12. She left everyone and everything that she had known her entire life to meet and marry a man that's she has not seen and knew next to nothing about. Her mentality had to be that because this was God she was going to do it. She believed it was the perfect will of God for her life. And they meshed perfectly.

The same can be true for you. God wants you to be a part of a power couple! He wants you to be like Acquila & Priscilla, with the church in their house. He wants you to be that couple where you're *both* doing exactly what he's called each of you to do, together. He doesn't want any one missing out on their assignment from God because of this relationship. In fact, he wants your relationship to be a major tool that helps both of you accomplish your life missions. (There are seasons to God-given assignments. So there might be a season where you're focused on your assignment more and then in the next season the focus shifts more to your spouses').

The point is that assignments match when this relationship is of God. If he feels like he's called to be a missionary to China and she feels like she's called to be an inner city worker in Detroit, no matter how great they may be as people, this relationship is not going to work. They may be attracted to each other. They may like each other. They may feel like this could be Bae. But if you're assignments don't match this probably isn't the one God had in mind for you.

God needs you to be a power couple working together to do what he's called you to do. This is why you need to interview, interview, interview, interview, interview. When you're dating, you've got to talk and talk and talk and talk and talk. And this is one reason why you need to know what God has assigned you to do & they need to know what they're assigned to do before you marry.

**Question #5: What does God say?**

When it's all said and done, God is the like the umpire in baseball. The umpire says when someone is safe or out. If God has a Bae for you, God knows who they are. That's one reason why it was so great that this servant stopped and prayed before he did anything else. You've got to pray throughout the dating process. You've got to ask "God, what do you say about this person? What do you say about this relationship? Is this the person for me?" You need to seek God's counsel throughout the process.

> The man bowed low and worshiped the Lord. "Praise the Lord, the God of my master, Abraham," he said. "The Lord has shown unfailing love and faithfulness to my master, for he has led me straight to my master's relatives." Genesis 24:22-27 NLT

You want to be able to say, "God led me to them" on your wedding day. He leads us through the Bible, he leads by the Holy spirit in your heart, you having a peace there. He leads by the inward voice and sometimes an even stronger voice in your heart, called the voice of the Holy Ghost. He, sometimes, leads by visions and dreams. You ultimately want to know that you know that this is the person God has for me because ultimately God knows what's best for you. He knows not only what what's best for you now, he knows what's going to be best for you five years from now, 10 years from now, 20 years now, for your kids, your grandkids. He sees all of this. He's already worked all of this out. So you want to follow his direction no matter what and marry the one he has in mind for you. The Holy Spirit will guide you to the love of your life.

# CHAPTER 4: BE PICKY!

One of my hopes for this book is that it requires you to step up your game. I don't want this to be type of teaching that just tickles your ears and gets you excited. I'm going to give you the truth and here is one piece of it. If you want God's best for you, you're going to have to become your best in God.

One of the problems that unmarried individuals can have is that we hold on to fallacies. We can fall into thinking that we can just stay the way we are and get God's best or that we can just settle for anyone that is fine or sexy and have a great marriage. We need to develop our character and we need to pick someone of great character as well.

That's why the title of this chapter is Be Picky! I'm not referring to being picky in regards to how they look as much as to their character.

When you start to talk with or date someone that you're attracted to you, typically put your best foot forward, right? So do they. When you meet them, they always look their best, and smell their best. They communicate well. They're selfless. She seems so sweet. He seems so strong. But what you see at first isn't necessarily real.

Have you ever experienced that? You think you're dating an angel and find out that you were dating the devil's spawn! So we need a way to be able to tell if she is really as sweet as she portrays herself to be, or is he really as strong as he seems to be? Is she what the Bible calls a rooftop woman? Is he a boy in men's clothes? These are questions that need to be answered.

> Beware of false prophets who come disguised as harmless sheep but are really vicious wolves. You can identify them by their fruit, that is, by the way they act. Can you pick grapes from thorn bushes, or figs from thistles? Matthew 7:15, 16 NLT

Now, of course, he's talking about prophets here, people that say that they're speaking on behalf of God. He's saying to beware of false prophets because they will come to you and present themselves to you as something that they're not. The same thing is actually true in dating as well. People who are trying to present themselves as sweet women or as strong men of God when they are not present themselves as harmless when actually they're very harmful. They present themselves as someone that is good and going to help you when they could actually ruin your life.

Well, how can you tell if someone is who they say they are? Once again, Jesus says here that you can identify by them their fruit, which simply means by the way they act. Notice that if he's telling you that you need to identify them, then clearly what's on the outside doesn't always match what's on the inside! What you're attempting to identify is what's on the inside. What's on the outside may be the complete opposite of what's on the inside.

> But the Lord said to Samuel, "Don't judge by his appearance or height, for I have rejected him. The Lord doesn't see things the way you see them. People judge by outward appearance, but the Lord looks at the heart." 1 Samuel 16:7 NLT

When Samuel went to anoint a new King of Israel, he came to Jesse's house and saw Jesse's sons. He saw his first born and he looked like a King. Samuel thought that this must be the guy. And God spoke to him and said, "Don't judge by his appearance or height." That might be a word for some ladies! "He got to be six, six." He could be six six, and as evil as Goliath! The Lord doesn't see things the way you see them. People often judge by outward appearance, but the Lord looks at the heart and God is saying that that is what we need to learn to do. You need to be able to identify the fake ones.

> "Who among you is wise and understanding? Let him show by his good behavior his deeds in the gentleness of wisdom." James 3:13 NASB

The way to tell whether somebody is sweet, or strong is by watching their behavior. That takes time. That's why you can't meet somebody tomorrow and get married next week. You can't run to Vegas or, here in Michigan, to Toledo! Even if you fully believe your relationship is from God, that you've met his Bae for you, that doesn't meant that you need to act on it immediately. There's a reason why the Bible says to prove all things when referring to supposed 'words from the Lord.' It's not that God doesn't speak and lead us, it's that not everything that we think came from God is. You need to give your relationship enough time to prove itself out.

## Be Picky About Character

Now, you may have heard from some family or friends that you're *too* picky. They may be right. If as a woman you're saying "Hey, if he's not 6'5, then I'm not going to date him." And then, God sends some guy that's only 6' and you turn him down because of it, that's being silly. If, as a man, you're saying "Hey, she has to have long hair" and she has short hair, but she's fine as can be. Yet you dismiss her. That's stupid. Okay? I'm not talking about being physically picky. That doesn't mean that you shouldn't be attracted to them. You definitely need to.

Once again, I'm talking about being picky in regards to their character. This is the second most important decision of your life. Whoever you hitch yourself to is going to have a huge impact on your life. And if they have good character, well, that's going to lead to good things, but if they have bad character then that's going to lead to bad things.

The Bible says the person that runs with the wise will be wise, but the person that runs with fools will be destroyed (Proverbs 13:20). You want to marry the wise person, not the fool. You want to marry a sweet woman, not a rooftop woman, the strong man, not the weak man.

The Bible does give us some more information about how to determine if the person that you're beign approached by, talking to or dating has the right character to be God's Bae for you. Let's begin to look at what the Bible says a sweet woman looks like by identifying what she doesn't look like.

> Better to dwell in a corner of a housetop, than in a house shared with a contentious woman. Proverbs 21:9 NKJV

One translation describes this as living alone in the corner of an attic. Remember when you were in school and someone in your class got in trouble. Its quite possible that the teacher made them go sit in the corner. He's saying it's better to be that person than to be in a nice, lovely, large home where there's plenty of space with *this* woman.

> Better to dwell in the wilderness, Than with a contentious and angry woman. Proverbs 21:19 NKJV

> A foolish son is the ruin of his father, And the contentions of a wife are a continual dripping. Proverbs 19:13 NKJV

A continual dripping is annoying like when someone runs their nails down a chalkboard! He's describing *life* with this type of woman!

> A continual dripping on a very rainy day and a contentious woman are alike; Whoever restrains her restrains the wind, And grasps oil with his right hand. Proverbs 27:15, 16 NKJV

In other words, it's impossible to know what she doing. You can't figure her out. You're in trouble, bro!

*Clearly, it's better to be single than be with the wrong woman.* God is telling single men what type of woman to avoid because marrying the wrong woman is awful.

## The Profile of a Contentious Woman

So what is a contentious woman? Because we saw that word over and over and over and over again. The Hebrew word translated contentious means brawling. It refers to someone that is constantly in strife with you. Some other words that's often used in describing this word are angry or vexation.

A more modern definition of contentious is 'causing or likely to cause an argument. A person that is *given* to arguing or provoking an argument.' So this is a person that's always coming at your throat. They just are touchy. You feel like you have to walk on eggshells around them because you never know what might set them off. You might sneeze the wrong way and get told off.

These type of women exist! And, unfortunately, the contentious woman is who our culture is trying to train our young women to be! A lot of the most popular artists and songs of our day promote this kind of behavior or worse. Some of the woman that are presented as role models today would surely qualify as the contentious woman in Bible days.

I believe God is saying to women today to *not* be that kind of woman. He's saying to single men, don't pursue that kind of woman. You don't want the women who is quick to snap at you, to put her hand on her hip, roll her neck and get with you. That's not what you want. You want a sweet woman.

In Judges 16, we read about the mighty Samson fully turning away from God. He wasn't necessarily the most dedicated man of God but he did honor some very important instructions that God had given him. What changed? He got with the wrong woman. Her name was Delilah.

If you remember the story, she was trying to get information from him for nefarious purposes. And she got it from him, the Bible said, "by pressing him daily with her words until he was vexed unto death." He finally gave in and it caused him to lose his eyes and his life. Its just that constant dripping. You don't want that!

One way to spot a contentious woman is to see if she's contentious with other people besides you. If she is, just give it some time, and she'll be contentious with you! If she's feuding with someone else or she's holding onto a grudge, that's a red flag, bro. Sure. She may struggle with some things and have to deal with it. But if she refuses to address it, if it has been going on for months or years, she's not ready yet.

In 1 Timothy 3 & 5, The Bible says that women are not to be slanderers or false accusers meaning that they are not supposed to be liars. It also teaches that they are not to be gossips. Those behaviors are the behaviors of contentious women.

Job's wife is another example of a contentious woman. When things got tough, she turned on him. I saw a picture on Instagram that jumped out at me one day. It said that a man's test of loyalty is when he's doing well in life. A woman's test of loyalty is when he's not. You want the type of woman that will stick by you when you aren't on top of the world.

In 1 Samuel 6, David was doing his best to get the ark of the covenant to Jerusalem. When he finally was pulling it off, he was dancing before God! You want the type that cheers you on even though she knows that you can't dance! You want the type that would say 'Dance, Baby Dance!" You don't want to be like his wife, Michal, and ridicule him for doing the best he can to honor God. That's not a sweet woman.

# CHAPTER 5: THE SWEET WOMAN

So what does a Sweet Woman look like? In 1 Peter 3, the Apostle is talking to women and he's teaching them that if they have a husband that's not obeying God's word, they can actually win him to God by their lifestyle.

Your lifestyle is that powerful. You can actually win a man to God. That doesn't mean you should go date and marry one that is far from God! He's talking to those who are already married to somebody! The point is that you can actually have that much influence on a man. You can also turn a man away from God, which is why men need to be careful to make sure they have the right woman because she *will* affect your character.

> Do not let your adornment be merely outward--arranging the hair, wearing gold, or putting on fine apparel— rather let it be the hidden person of the heart, with the incorruptible beauty of a gentle (KJV - meek) and quiet spirit, which is very precious in the sight of God.  1 Peter 3:3, 4 NKJV

Notice that the word adornment is referring to your decorations or simply what people see when they look at you. God is saying to women, "Don't let what people see when they look at you or even think about you be only how beautiful you are. He wasn't saying you shouldn't wear makeup or nice clothes. He wasn't saying that you shouldn't look attractive. God created women to be beautiful. But He is saying here to not let that be what you're known for.. Instead of be known for your character more than you are for your beauty.

The King James version of this verse uses the phrase 'meek & quiet spirit.' The word meek means "humble & mild." The word quiet here means "still, undisturbed and undisturbing." This is a great description of a sweet woman. She's humble and that is gold! Whether you're talking about a man or a woman. You want to avoid the person with a case of the "I's." "I did this." "I did that." "I am this." "I am that." If you count all the eyes in a conversation and she breaks a world record you need to run like Usain Bolt!

**Humility is Attractive**

You want somebody that is humble. Someone that has an appropriate view of themselves. Romans 12:3 talks about not thinking of yourself as though are you more than you are. That doesn't mean that you aren't great, valuable and special. You are all those things. But at the same time, pride sells a lie whereas humility believes the truth. The truth is you are all of those things because of God not just because of yourself. You are all of those things because of the people that God has placed in your life to help develop you. You may have made some right decisions in life but that doesn't make you better than everyone else.

Notice that you can actually see the hidden man of our heart by observing if she is meek, if she is undisturbed and undisturbing. The rooftop woman is disturbed partly because of her fear. She's afraid she's going to be mistreated. She may feel like she's got to do this herself, that she has protect herself so that she can have her way in the world.

She's touchy which means she's actually quickly disturbed, where this sweet woman is more mature. She's undisturbed. She doesn't get moved so easily. Her faith, her confidence is in God. And she's undisturbing, she's not the one that's a continual dripping - constantly messing with & causing problems for you. No, she is peaceable.

God says that this individual, this type of spirit is very precious in his sight. God sees this sweet woman as very valuable. This is similar to what we find in Proverbs 31. The Bible says about that virtuous woman that her price is far above rubies. Clearly, this is the kind of woman that a man wants to find. This is Bae-territory here!

> For in this manner (way), in former times, the holy women who trusted in God also adorned themselves, being sub-missive to their own husbands, as Sarah obeyed Abraham, calling him lord, whose daughters you are if you do good and are not afraid with any terror. (NLT - You are her daugh-ters when you do what is right without fear of what your husbands might do.) 1 Peter 3:5, 6 NKJV

The key phrase in this scripture may be that they 'trusted in God.' The reason why a sweet woman can be this way is because she has a trust in God. Not in men. Not in that her husband is always right. No, it is in the fact that even if he's wrong, because she's trusting in God and acting in faith, God will handle it.

Listen, it doesn't matter who you're with. They're going to make mistakes. They're going to go the wrong direction from time to time. And guess what? If you were in charge, you would too. It's just human nature. But because she's able to trust in God, she's un-disturbed and undisturbing.

Remember, the Bible says they adorned themselves in this way, meaning this is how they were. This wasn't something they were able to do from time to time, this was their character. There is

---

a difference between a woman who can be sweet and a sweet woman.

When you have a meek and quiet spirit, you're able to be submissive to your own husband. Why? Because you recognize that God's got you. I love a book that was written a years ago by Bunny Wilson called 'Liberated through Submission.' She tells a story about how she went on this journey from being the contentious rooftop woman, who was constantly contending with her man, to realizing, through her relationship with God, that that was the wrong approach. She found herself unhappy with how her life and marriage were going so she shifted to becoming a sweet woman & discovered that there is actually freedom in submitting to the person God has called you to be submitted to.

Submission does not mean being under someone's feet. It doesn't mean that we, as a couple, don't have conversations about major decisions that we may be facing. It just means that at the end of the conversation, he gets to make the final decision. And his wife submits to it.

Submission is not agreement. However, when you submit to a decision that you don't agree with, you take the position that you will fully support his decision and if he ends up being wrong, *we* were wrong. It means that you are undisturbed and undisturbing because ultimately your faith is in God. When a man knows that his woman has his back like that he can confidently step out and do what he believes God wants him to do.

Notice that a woman has to adorn herself with these things. A man can't and shouldn't beat her over the head with these scriptures saying "Submit! Submit! Submit!" She's got to choose to have this kind of character like Sarah did.

**The Picture of a Sweet Woman**

Sarah is specifically chosen by God as an example for women. Why? Her husband came to her with a crazy, God-inspired dream and she allowed him to chase it. She allowed her man to take her away from everything she knew without knowing where they were going and she didn't drive him crazy. She didn't fight him. She believed in him. And when he experienced God's miracles, when they were made very rich, when they had the miracle baby and even now enjoy eternal fame, she enjoyed the rewards along with him because they did it together. She's a great example for women who are single or married to study. *Sweet women don't let fear run their life.*

So why do some women act like rooftop women? One, because of arrogance, they actually think they are better than their spouse or are of an superior intellect. And that's a problem. No matter how brilliant you are you must be humble enough to realize that nobody has all the answers by themselves.. Two is simply a lack of self control. They allow their emotions to determine their behavior. They just lose it & everyone around them has to deal with the consequences. These are issues that arise when you don't have a personal relationship with God.

When I say relationship, I don't just mean to pray a prayer every once in a while. I mean actually reading your Bible everyday, praying everyday, going to church, getting in a small group, serving consistently. I mean being a mature Christian. It's impossible for a woman to be (or stay a sweet woman) in this crazy world, where people and life will constantly test and try to change you, without this relationship with God.

Here's another great picture of a sweet women.

> Who can find a virtuous wife for her worth is far above rubies. The heart of her husband safely trust her; So he will have no lack of gain. (The New Living Translation says she will greatly enrich his life). She does him good and not

evil all the days of her life. She also rises while it is yet night and provides food for her household and a portion for her maidens. She extends her hands to the poor. Yes. She reaches out to her hands to the needy. She opens her mouth were wisdom. And in her tongue is the law of kindness. Proverbs 31:10-12, 15, 20, 26 NKJV

Notice that when the Bible described this woman, it talks about her husband, her children, her household, the poor and how she uses her words. So this is a woman who is other-focused. She is kind and selfless. She's taking care of a husband. She's taking care of her household. She takes care of people in need. Even in choosing her words, she takes care of other people. That is a sweet woman. Man of God, that's what you're looking for!

# CHAPTER 6 THE STRONG MAN

Now let's talk about what a Strong Man looks like.

In 1 Timothy 3, God is talking about a man who wants to have hold the office of a Bishop, which is an overseer of men. God gives a lists of qualifications that he actually expects every man to meet before he's allowed to be a leader of men. He's revealing what a Man's character should look like. If a man doesn't consistently demonstrate this type of character, God is saying that he's not qualified for promotion.

So this chapter is perfect for revealing to us what a Strong Man looks like and what a Strong man doesn't look like. Woman of God, you want to pay attention to this!

> So an elder must be a man whose life is above reproach. He must be faithful to his wife. He must exercise self-control, live wisely, and have a good reputation. He must enjoy having guests in his home, and he must be able to teach. He must not be a heavy drinker or be violent. He must be gentle, not quarrelsome, and not love money. 1 Timothy 3:2-3 NLT

Let's break this down. He must live a clean life. He must be faithful to his wife (of course that refers to a married man attempting to qualify for this position). He must exercise self control, not society control (because he's committing crimes and the police have to be called to control him). Not God-control. Self-control. He must live wisely and have a good reputation. He's ready and willing to teach others and he's hospitable, which means he's a giver. he's self-less not selfish.

He must not be a heavy drinker (or a drinker of alcohol at all really, remember that Proverbs 31 says its not for kings to drink strong drink) or be violent. So he's not given to intoxication, not just from alcohol or weed or any other substance that can be abused in his life.

If he's smoking weed, gambling, watching porn etc. he's *not* a strong man. He's a weak man. Any man can do those things. It takes a strong man to overcome those temptations. He can have all the size and muscles in the world but if his character is weak, he is a weak man.

A man can be both strong physically and weak. He can be a boy in a man's body. As a woman, you're trying to look on the inside to determine if he's a strong man.

Notice that he must not be quarrelsome. In other words, just like there is a rooftop woman there is a rooftop man. I like to call them hot heads. Everything that we read about the rooftop woman applies to men too! You don't want a hot head. If he's a hot head, he is not a strong man. He can't control himself! He can't handle his emotions.

**You Don't Want a Hot Head**

I was in a basketball league about a year or so ago. The team that I'm on, we've won lots of championships, but now all of us are a little older. So we started adding some young guys to our teams so that we can keep winning. Makes sense, right? So we had one guy on our team that was ridiculously talented. Honestly, I haven't been on a court with many that are better. And He was doing his thing and really carrying our team. But we got in a close game. And you know, of course, when you're in a game against other guys and you're dominating them, they will mess with you. They will try to get in your head because they know that can't stop you. So that's what they did.

And at the end of the game, he lost it and cost us the game. I mean, he just acted like a hot head. All the older guys tried to calm him down but he just couldn't get it together. Now he was young, clearly not at a stage in life where marriage was really an option for him, but sometimes women make the mistake of dating or even marrying a man who has yet to grow out of this.

And you see this a lot in men today. You'll see this today in the NFL. In fact, I saw it yesterday in a college football game. Some guy just got hot and starts punching at a guy with his bare fists even though the other guy had a helmet on. Hot head. You don't want to marry that man. Someone that's quick to yell at you, someone that barks at you... that's a weak man. He's not ready.

> He must be gentle, not quarrelsome, and not love money. 1 Timothy 3:3 NLT

He's not chasing money. He's not chasing after whatever the latest get rich quick scheme is. He's not willing to bend the rules to enrich himself.

Listen, you want a solid guy. Clean life, loves God, selfless, self-controlled. He's a man's man. He's got everything that makes him a man but he's solid, not wild and crazy. *You want the solid man not the wild man.*

Sometimes women go after the bad boy. That's a silly woman. She's not ready yet. You don't want the bad boy and you'll probably figure that out the wrong way. You want the good guy with an edge. You want a man's man wih God's heart. That's what you want. You don't want the bad guy with a little good. That's not a strong man. That's a weak man.

Anybody can lose their temper. Anybody can smoke and drink and just party and look at porn. Anyone can sleep around. Anybody can lust after every attractive woman that they see. You need to ask yourself "Is he strong enough to watch his eyes." When you go out in public with him is it like taking a puppy out. A puppy just pees everywhere with no regard for what's appropriate. Is he like that with his eyes, taking in every attractive woman while with you.

It's a weak man that can't control himself sexually. Is he strong enough to keep his zipper up? Is he trying to sleep with you? If so, he's not a Strong Man. His flesh is running his life. His desires are running his life.

It doesn't matter if this can hurt your relationship. It doesn't matter if you could get an STD. It doesn't matter if we could have an unplanned pregnancy. It doesn't matter that this could lead to emotional hurt and pain. None of that matters. All that matters is that he wants you. That's a weak man. You don't want that. In fact, that's not a man, that's a boy in man's body.

Is he cynical? Or is he optimistic? Anybody can be a cynic. Anybody can be critical. Anybody can have a little attitude about everything in the world. Anyone can be bitter. Every generation has it's challenges but I see this one a little bit more in the younger generation. Too many seem to be cynical and know-it-alls. Anybody can do that. Does he have enough strength to still have some optimism, to have dreams, to believe in others?

Is he strong enough to follow God even when it's hard? You don't want to hook yourself to a train that may go off track at the first sign of trouble. When you get married to somebody (especially as a woman) you are hooking yourself to their life. Where they go in life will have a major impact on you.

> Watch ye, stand fast in the faith, quit you like men, be strong. 1 Corinthians 16:13 KJV

Paul is telling men here to be vigilant because we have an enemy out here looking to harm us and our families. He says to "Quit you like men" which means to be manly. How do I do that? What does it mean to be manly?

> Be of good courage, and let us play the men for our people, and for the cities of our God: and the LORD do that which seemeth him good. 2 Samuel 10:12 KJV

This opening of scripture is talking to people about to go into battle. The men are being told to not surrender. They are being told that even though it looked bad, they should man up and fight anyway.

This is the kind of situation where you find out what people are made of. They were surrounded. They had the enemy in front of them and the enemy behind them. And there was a strategy being discussed. And part of the strategy was for them to "play the men."

Clearly, there is a way men act in tough times. Strong men don't wilt. They may not feel great. They may be afraid. They may be knocked down, but they don't just stay down. They get up. A man can get beat down, and still get up on one leg and say "I'm not stopping. You're going to have to kill me." That's how a man acts when what is at stake is his family, his people and his God.

The three Hebrew boys in Daniel 3 who said, when threatened with being thrown into a fiery furnace for not bowing down to a false God, "God will protect us. But even if he doesn't we still won't bow" those are strong men.  When things get tough is he going to throw his Bible away, stop trying, and stop following God's plan for his life. Is he going to give up and go back to smoking, drinking, gambling, doing his thing?  Can he stand up in the worst moments of his life and still be the man God created him to be?

I'm not talking about people not making mistakes. There's a difference between somebody who's struggling with something. And then this being their character. We started off by simply saying, you will know them by how they act, by their behavior. That's a pattern of action. As you watch them for a while who do they continue to show themselves to be? Who is he when things are tough, when he's tired, when he's frustrated, when he's angry, because that's the real him. That's when you know if he's a strong man or nah.

## Strong Men have a Relationship with God

A man can't truly be a strong man without a relationship with God.

> A wise man is strong; yea, a man of knowledge increaseth strength. Proverbs 24:5 KJV

What makes you a wise man? The word of God. When a man has daily Bible time and is listening to the word of God being preached to him consistently, he's planting Word of God into his heart and can be the strong man. When he's connected with other godly men that he allows to help him maintain strong character, he's in position to become a strong man.

As an athlete, the thing I probably miss the most about playing was the camaraderie of the teams that I was on. You know, just being on a bus with a bunch of dudes acting crazy, having fun. I played basketball at Bible College and so I remember moments where the Holy spirit fell in the bus!

You know that involvement in a brotherhood is not supposed to stop. You may no longer experience that because you're on a sports team but you're still supposed to be a part of a team, a team of men helping each other to live this life the way God wants us to. A guy who doesn't have that with the right friends is vulnerable to weakness. It's going to be hard for him to stay strong. Even if he goes to church, he still needs to do life together with wise men to be wise and strong.

Woman of God, if you have to get him to go to church, if he's only going because of you or your encouragement, then he's not a strong man! He's not ready for you! (If he just started going, he's not ready yet either. Stop shopping in the nursery!)

Everyone can see this world. Everyone can see that everything in this world has been created. The Bible says everyone knows God, that he exists. However, not everyone is happy that he does. They reject him because they would rather be their own god rather than serve the true God. And if he's still in his own "god phase", you don't want to be with that. A strong man is strong enough to be able to recognize that he is not God, that the God of the Bible is God. He makes the decision to worship and serve him. You want that kind of man.

This man that we're talking about fears God, he's strong. He's selfless. He's a server. Jesus came to serve not to be served. Just because you're a leader doesn't mean that you're not the servant. The leader is supposed to serve.

One of the things that I can say, about myself, I've got things I'm growing in, but my household knows that I'm the one that's going to serve everybody. And that didn't happen overnight. I had to train myself to think like that because real leaders are servant leaders. And you want to watch for that as a women. When you're dating or talking to a guy, is he always waiting for you to serve him or is he the type to try to find a way to serve you? And not just you, but his mom, his family, his friends.

Remember, we're talking about a pattern of behavior. We know there are moments, but I'm talking about his pattern. Does He lead with kindness? Is he diligent? Can he provide for you? Is he diligent enough to be able to bring the money in.

> Love endures long and is patient and kind; love never is envious nor boils over with jealousy, is not boastful or vain-glorious, does not display itself haughtily. It is not connected (arrogant and inflated with pride); it is not rude (unman-nerly) and does not act unbecomingly. Love (God's love in us) does not insist on its own rights or its own way, for it is not self-seeking; it is not touchy or fretful or resentful; it takes no account of the evil done to is (it pays no attention to a suffered wrong). It does not rejoice at injustice and unrighteousness, but rejoices when right and truth prevail. Love bears up under anything and everything that comes, is ever ready to believe the best of every person, its hopes are fadeless under all circumstances, and it endures everything (without weakening). Love never fails (never fades out or becomes obsolete or comes to an end.) 1 Corinthians 13:4-8 AMPC

Can you plug in the person's name that you're talking about dating everywhere where it says love? Can you plug in your own name? If you're going to get that person that is sweet or that person that is strong, you go have to become this person and be able to plug your name in here as well. Ultimately, you want to be with someone who wants to love God and others with you!

Discovering the truth about the character of the individual you are considering is key to identifying if they are a Bae or Nah. Use the word of God to help you to determine whether she's a sweet or rooftop woman, whether he's a strong or a weak man and one day you walk down the aisle getting ready to get married to Bae!

# CHAPTER 7: NO MORE GAMES

D ating is just not supposed to be as hard as people complain that it is. It's not supposed to be as difficult as it seems. Sometimes it is so difficult because we're doing it wrong. The world has its way of dating but God has a different way. If you're a Christian you need to date God's way. If you attempt to date the world's way and yet think you're going to find God's person you're going to be in for a rude awakening.

In this chapter, I want to show you a way to date that honors God, that does right by others, and yet can lead you to Bae.

Let's go back to Genesis 24. Remember this is where we find the story of how Isaac and Rebekah found each other. Now as we discussed, in this time, things were very, very different. And so Abraham sent his servant to find a wife for Isaac. He had a very specific criteria that he wanted him to use in identifying her. God already had somebody in mind for Isaac and God orchestrated things so that Isaac and Rebekah could be together! I want you to notice some of the things that his servant did, because I think that they actually translate to dating today.

Before he had finished praying... Genesis 24:15a

That's a good start. Isn't it? If you're interested in dating you need to start with prayer!

> ...he saw a young woman named Rebekah coming out with her water jug on her shoulder. She was the daughter of Bethuel, who was the son of Abraham's brother Nahor and his wife, Milcah. Genesis 24:15b

If you remember, Abraham asked for him to find somebody that was from his family line. And so here, She checks off that box!

> Rebekah was very beautiful and old enough to be married, but she was still a virgin. She went down to the spring, filled her jug, and came up again. Running over to her, the servant said, "Please give me a little drink of water from your jug." Genesis 24:16, 17

Clearly, he's looking for somebody that's attractive for Isaac. So when he sees her, he immediately recognizes that she's gorgeous and approaches her.

> The servant watched her in silence, wondering whether or not the LORD had given him success in his mission. Genesis 24:21 NLT

Notice that he didn't just see and approach a beautiful woman. He evaluated her. Remember what he had asked God. He had prayed to God to help him identify the woman that God had in mind for Isaac by her not only giving him water but offering to give water to his camels. And Rebekah did! As we already mentioned, he finds out that Rebekah is from Abraham's family line and eventually is brought to her father and uncle. He tells them the story of how he met her and why he's there in verse 48.

> Then I bowed low and worshiped the Lord. I praised the

> Lord, the God of my master, Abraham, because he had led me straight to my master's niece to be his son's wife. 49. So tell me—will you or won't you show unfailing love and faithfulness to my master? Please tell me yes or no, and then I'll know what to do next." Genesis 24:48, 49 NLT

Notice he states his intention. "I'm here to get a wife for Isaac." In a new relationship it is vitally important to state your intentions and get clarity about the other person's intentions as well. We'll talk a little more about that later. I also want you to notice that although God led him to Rebekah, she and her family still had a choice to make. They could choose to not have her marry Isaac. Remember that after Abraham had told his servant that an Angel would lead him to the woman God had in mind, if she decided not to come, his servant would be free of his oath.

Just because God has somebody in mind for you doesn't mean that they are required to be with you. Everybody has choice, right? Everyone has been given free will by God. God will not violate anyone's free will. Of course, Rebekah says yes!

> One evening as he was walking and meditating in the fields, he looked up and saw the camels coming. When Rebekah looked up and saw Isaac, she quickly dismounted from her camel. "Who is that man walking through the fields to meet us?" she asked the servant. And he replied, "It is my master." So Rebekah covered her face with her veil. Then the servant told Isaac everything he had done. And Isaac brought Rebekah into his mother Sarah's tent, and she became his wife. He loved her deeply, and she was a special comfort to him after the death of his mother. Genesis 24:63-67 NLT

Although things were done differently then, Rebekah was clearly the one God had in mind for Isaac. She was used by God to comfort him after his mother's death, they had miracle babies and more.

So let's back up a little and revisit some of the things that we identified in this story that we can apply to dating today.

## Approach Her

The servant first saw her beauty and approached her. Remember when you were in elementary school and if a boy liked a girl, he'd hit her or be mean to her. Yeah? Well, we're not in elementary school anymore. If you're attracted to a girl, step up! Sometimes Christian guys get so spiritual (actually I like to use the word spooky) that we see a woman that we think is fine but want to watch her for 7.8 years before we approach her! It's like we're waiting for the Lord to cause the heavens to open, that we need to hear from God and know she's the one before we say hi!

You can get so spooky that you feel like something special has to happen before you approach a girl. Let me help you! It doesn't! There's a natural side and a supernatural side to every blessing from God. The natural side may just be you saying Hi!

Another issue that some struggle with is that they are afraid of what people will say about them. They're afraid that they will get a negative reputation for trying to get to know a number of different women. At some point you have to get past what people say and just make sure that you are doing things the right way (we'll talk about that way in a moment) and let God deal with other people.

## Evaluate Them

It's okay if you're attracted to someone, to approach and try to get to know them. You need to do that so that you can do the next thing that Abraham's servant did. Evaluate them. Now, sometimes what you'll do is you will meet someone that you're attracted to and has potential to be Bae and you might not approach right away. You might want to watch them from a distance. You might want to go out with a group of friends and see how they act. You might want to see if they are someone that is a giver or a taker. You may want to evaluate if she is a sweet woman or he a strong man.

That's really what the dating process is all about. Evaluating this person that you're interested in. You're trying to see their character. And in the servant's case, that's exactly what he was trying to do. That's why he asked that God send a woman who would not only give him water but would actually go out of her way to give water to his camels. He knew that any woman that would give him water and then volunteer to give water to his camels was a sweet woman.

**State Your Intentions**
Here is something very important. It is key to dating God's way. He stated his intentions. Now I normally get some female amens when I mention this because this is an issue that many women have with the dating world today. They find that guys will engage with them in an ongoing friendship/relationship and they don't really know what he's there for. He's too much of a coward to say why he's entered this relationship with them or he's playing games with their emotions.

For example, I watched one relationship where a very eligible and successful Christian guy entered a relationship with a beautiful young single woman. They were talking by phone, Facetiming, visiting each other etc. on a regular basis and she started to fall for him. But he never stepped up and let her know his intentions. This left an open door for him so that if he stopped calling or met someone that he felt was a better fit for him, he could deny that they even had a romantic relationship. He could say he was just being her friend. He would have plausible deniability.

Well, She waited months for him to step up and he never planned to. She had to fend off bitter disappointment due to her having hopes and dreams of their possible life together (we'll talk about how to avoid this later) and in the meantime, she may have missed out on the one God had for her.

This is wrong! Love wouldn't do that to someone. And men aren't the only ones who do this. Women do too! God's way of dating is to state your intentions. That also means that women need to be clear about if a guy is wasting his time on you because you don't have any real interest in him. It is wrong to string him along just because you like the attention that he gives you.

> Since Jacob was in love with Rachel, he told her father, "I'll work for you for seven years if you'll give me Rachel, your younger daughter, as my wife." So Jacob worked seven years to pay for Rachel. But his love for her was so strong that it seemed to him but a few days. Genesis 29:18, 20 NLT

Here is another well known Bible love story. The story of Jacob and Rachel. Now Jacob had only been at Rachel's home for about a month. It only took a month for him to fall for her. And you know you're in love when you tell somebody that you will work for seven years just to be with them. The Bible says that although it was years to Jacob it seemed like days. Notice that they weren't sleeping together. This wasn't about sex. This was about love.

I want you to notice that when a man wants you, he will move heaven and earth to get you. He will chase you. If you have to chase him, there's something wrong. Jacob so wanted Rachel that he came up with this idea! He decided that he loved her so much that he would offer his services seven years to have her. This is what real men do!

That's why when a women comes across a guy that won't state his intentions that's a red flag. A real man will move heaven or hell to be with you. At some point, early in your friendship, he's going to make a decision to really come after you.

> The man who finds a wife finds a treasure, and he receives favor from the LORD. Proverbs 18:22 NLT

He's treasure hunting. What would you do if somebody you trust told you about a $10 million treasure that everyone is searching for and you found it? You would dig it up! And once you had it you wouldn't be searching anymore. Right? The Bible talks about that in the book of Matthew, how a man found a field and in the field he found a treasure. So then he went and sold everything he had to buy that field. And that's really a picture of what happens when a man is really truly interested in a woman. He's done searching, he's ready to dump everything so he can get this treasure.

If he's not there yet, if you find yourself saying that "he don't respond to my text messages" or "he isn't consistent." It's because he's not that into you. Come on, let me help you. Can I help you? Let me help you. If he's not moving heaven and earth, he don't want you. And you don't want to be with him if he don't want you.

Now I know that men and women are different to some degree. Sometimes, a guy can kind of talk his way into a relationship with a woman. She may leave the door open to a relationship with him by saying that's she willing to get to know him with the intention of discovering if she would like to commit to a relationship with him.

However, that's not how guys are in general. You're not going to change his mind about chasing you. It doesn't work like that. He might be attracted to you. He might be intrigued by you, but he probably already knows very early that you aren't it for him. That's why he's inconsistent. He might play some games with you. He might use you to meet an emotional need or a physical need. However, he already knows that you're not what he's looking for. So he'll maintain this relationship with you while he's looking for something better.

## You Deserve Better

Don't you let anybody treat you like a backup. Don't you let anybody put you on hold! He's not saying "I have found treasure!" and if he isn't then you need to end that relationship. To somebody you walk on water. To somebody, you are *it*. When they meet & get to know you, they are excited about you. They will do whatever it takes to be with you.

Now, I can imagine someone reading this book and saying. "Well, that could change pastor." First of all, if it changes, you will know. There is no point in you sitting there thinking about it and wondering about this relationship until you do know his clear intentions. You have to stop imagining a future together with somebody that you're not sure even wants to have a future with you.

Sometimes what people do is have whole romances in their head with someone that they haven't even gone on a date with! They have worked out an entire movie plot and he hasn't even asked you out yet! He hasn't even told you that he's interested. You can't let yourself go there mentally or emotionally until it's clear he wants you badly.

"Well, Pastor, he's just kind of weak. He just needs a little extra help." That's not a strong man. That's a weak man. That's an indecisive man. Why would you want that? And most of the time, it just isn't true. Ask any guy that you respect these questions, "When you see something you want, do you go after it? Is there anything that's going to keep you from it?"

Let me say it this way. You are the answer to somebody's prayer. So don't you beg for love. Don't sell yourself short by pursuing somebody that doesn't really want to be with you.

You need someone who can't wait to talk to you and spend time with you and get to know you and fall in love with you. So stop selling short for half-hearted, lukewarm, hesitant and indecisive. It's so much better to be alone and be with someone who makes you feel alone.

You want to marry someone who sees being with you like winning the lottery. As Tony Gaskin says, "Want who wants you. You can't make someone want you. Don't chase someone who is committed to running from you."

I love something else that I read "the best piece of dating advice I've ever received is this. If they like, you you'll know it, if they don't, you'll be confused. Honestly it's all you need to know."

Nona Jones says "If somebody is not interested in you don't internalize another person's choice as an assessment of your value because they don't want to be with you. It doesn't mean you're not worth being with. It just means they don't want to be with you and they could just be missing out."

> It is not conceited (arrogant and inflated with pride); it is not rude (unmannerly) and does not act unbecomingly. Love (God's love in us) does not insist on its own rights or its own way, for it is not self-seeking; it is not touchy or fretful or resentful; it takes no account of the evil done to it (it pays no attention to a suffered wrong). 1 Corinthians 13:5 AMPC

Let no one seek his own, but each one the other's well-being. 1 Corinthians 10:24 NKJV

Love is not self-seeking. If love is not self-seeking then whose is it seeking? Its focused on what benefits other people. This is something to apply in dating. As Christians, we're supposed to love people. So we pray for people because we love people, right? We give, because we love people. When people treat us wrong, we find a way to do right, because we choose to walk in love. And when you're dating someone, love would not lead a person on. Let me say it again. Love would not lead people on.

## Dating is Not a Game

Dating is not a game because people's hearts involved. You can hurt people, deeply. So early in your friendship you need to state something like this "I'm going to be upfront with you about what I'm thinking, what I'm trying to accomplish, because I'm not interested in wasting your time or wasting mine. I'm not interested in breaking your heart or breaking mine. So these are my intentions. If I get to a place where I feel like this isn't really going to work, I will let you know as soon as possible so that neither one of us is being strung along."

Love doesn't play with people's emotions. Love doesn't break people's hearts. Love doesn't lead people on. Remember that.

# CHAPTER 8: THE RIGHT WAY TO DATE

So let's break down the right way to date in God's eyes.

## Chase (& Be Caught)

> The man who finds a wife finds a treasure, and he receives favor from the LORD. Proverbs 18:22 NLT

It's the man's job to pursue. It's *he* that finds a wife, not *she* that finds a husband. You see, God's way is the best way. One reason why people get hurt is because they stop following God's plan. It's important to allow the man to be the Hunter. That's how he's wired. He wants to hunt. He wants to pursue.

If you approach him and pursue him, you already gotten a mark against you. He already doesn't respect or value you the way that he really should. Also, you're positioning yourself to have him play games with you. If he really wanted you, he would have pursued you. But now he can use you to meet his emotional or physical need and then leave you when he finds someone that he does want to pursue.

In Judges 21 we find an interesting story that I think helps illustrate my point. Now the context here is that there has been a battle and there is a concern that the tribe of Benjamin will eventually be wiped out if they aren't allowed to have wives to have children with.

> Therefore they instructed the children of Benjamin, saying, "Go, lie in wait in the vineyards, and watch; and just when the daughters of Shiloh come out to perform their dances, then come out from the vineyards, and every man catch a wife for himself from the daughters of Shiloh; then go to the land of Benjamin. "And the children of Benjamin did so; they took enough wives for their number from those who danced, whom they caught. Then they went and returned to their inheritance, and they rebuilt the cities and dwelt in them. Judges 21:20-21, 23 NKJV

Obviously, today we would call this kidnapping but it was a different time. The men were told to hide in the vineyards and when the women come out to do their dances, catch you a wife. So that's what the men did! They had to quickly identify, and approach those women, didn't they?! If a man saw a beautiful girl, he knew that his friends saw her too. He knew that whoever got to her first was going to get to marry her. He knew that he was going to have to move or he was going to have to end up spending the rest of his life hanging out with his best friend who was married to this fine woman that he wanted!

Can you imagine this scene? These guys are hiding and in starting position while these women, suspecting nothing are just doing their dances to the Lord. They are just serving God. (By the way that is how this works for ladies, God tends to send your Bae when you're busy serving him. It worked for Ruth. She served God and God sent her Boaz!) And then here come these men coming out of the brush, running at them!

Notice that that it wasn't the women in the brush trying to identify and chase these men. That seems to be a picture of where we
are today. Women lusting after men's workout pictures, jumping
in their DM's and more! Listen, if you're trying to catch a man
you're doing it wrong! The best way is to let the man catch you.

The other side of that of course is that you do need to let him
catch you. This is, to some degree, a competition. If you play
games with men, they will eventually find someone else. They
want someone that wants to be with them badly too and they
should have that.

I heard a woman say something about this that made me laugh.
She was talking about the games she used to play. How a guy
would text her and she would let a couple of days go by before
she got back to him. I thought "all of these women are dancing
everywhere (doing their dance before the Lord) and you're having
him wait days just to text him back." You're playing games. Eventually, he will come to the conclusion that you're not interested
and find someone who clearly is.

I'm not saying that if you're interested that you should just come
out and say "I think you're fine, I think you're sexy. I want to
marry you" on the first day that you meet! Okay? But if you are
interested, at some point you have to show that interest.

## Communicate

Can two walk together, unless they are agreed.

Amos 3:3 NKJV

For there to be agreement there must be communication.

One of the things that has to happen in a dating relationship is that the couple needs to talk and come into agreement concerning the status of the relationship.

I came across a post online where a guy was talking about the stages of dating. He mentioned the talking stage (where we're just getting to know each other), the dating stage (getting to know each other while going on dates) & the relationship stage (all of the above just exclusive). Well, those stages may be mean different things to different people, right? Some people might say that "if we're talking with each other we shouldn't be in the talking stage with anyone else." Other people may say "we are not exclusive until, we say we're exclusive." So how do you know what people are thinking when everybody has different definitions for things, when everybody has different ideas of how this is supposed to work? You talk about it.

This is why I mentioned earlier about a man stating his intentions. If he takes the lead and says, "Hey, right now I'm just getting to know people. I just want to be friends." What does that look like? You need to have a conversation about that. Or if he's saying, "I'm interested in you." You can have that conversation. Or if she's saying, "Hey, I'm not really interested in dating right now. I just want to have some friends." Okay. Now he knows where she stands and can decide if he wants to pursue a friendship with her.

The point is that the conversation has to be had. That's one of the things that helps people to not get their heart broken. Also, it helps you not to lead somebody on when you take the time to actually communicate what you are thinking about this relationship. Let me reitrate that this conversation needs to happen early in the relationship.

## Cut Them Loose (When Necessary)

> To everything there is a season, a time for every purpose under heaven. A time to gain and a time to lose a time to keep and a time to throw away. Ecclesiastes 3:1, 6 KJV

In your relationship you should be evaluating each other and the relationship. If you reach a place where you realize that this isn't Bae, this isn't God's plan for you, you should end the relationship quickly. I'm going to say it again. When you realize this isn't it. End it. That doesn't mean there's anything wrong with them. They just might not be the person for you.

We talked earlier about some of the things that you're looking for in dating, and one of the things is do your assignments match, right? You feel like you're called to China. She feels like she's called to work in the inner city of Detroit. Once you both figure that out this relationship needs to change, right? We're not dating for marriage at this point. "I need to let you go so that you can find a person that wants to go to China with you", right? So when you realize this isn't it, you need to step up and end it.

I know that's easier said than done because your emotions are involved. This is one reason why these kinds of things should happen relatively early in a relationship. You should be talking about important things early in the process. The dating process really is an interview process. So even on the first date, you should definitely do something fun but you also have to make sure that you spend a lot of time talking.

As you get to know each other you can see if they check off the important things on your list. If you've got five things that are really important to you (such as their God-given assignment) and they are only two of those things this relationship probably should not last long.

You can't just keep dating someone because they are cute! You can't just keep dating someone because you love how they talk to you, how they smell or because they are sexy. Love is not self-seeking. You've got to be mature enough to not put yourself or them in a position where someone could get hurt because of your selfish desires. When you realize this isn't it. You've got to let them know this isn't it. Even if you're not sure, you need to communicate that so that no one is caught off guard.

When you know this is not God's plan for you both, let them go. Let them pursue God's will for their life, put them in position to be with the person that God has for them.

Once again, this is one reason why it's so wrong when people lead people on because what you've done is you've had them stop their life waiting for you when you know that they're not what you want. You're harming them.

I've watched celebrities do this to people. And I'll be honest with you. I've done this myself. When I graduated high school, there was this girl that I was friends with but the relationship changed over the summer. We went from kind of knowing each other to being on the phone every night for hours. We started to hang out and I started to develop feelings for her, and she clearly had feelings for me.

However, at that time I was probably a little too serious about everything and so I started asking myself a question. "Could I see myself marrying this girl?" And I just didn't think I could because I didn't think she was cute enough. I'm just being real. She was not somebody that I thought was gorgeous. She was somebody that was cute and so I was kind of trying to talk myself into thinking that she might be cute enough.

However, because I was stuck in this might-be stage, I never stated my full intentions. I never said, "I'm interested in you in this way." I never said, "I want to date you." I never say any of that stuff. But I talked to her like I was, and I hung out with her like I was, and then I went away to college and I didn't really talk to her.

Soon I started getting love letters from her that I never bothered to respond to. Well, I was just a jerk. I didn't really intend to be, but what I should've done was state my intentions and as soon as I realized that this relationship didn't have a future I should have cut all that stuff off. Instead, I hurt her and I regret it.

Now, don't throw this book away! You know you've made some mistakes too! My point is that when you look at them and you say, "Hey, they are cute but they're not what I really want" or "I don't think our assignments match" or "They're just not as mature as I need" or whatever it is, cut it off. Release them because there's somebody that when they meet them, they are going to think that they are one in a million.

## Be Chaste

> Flee sexual immorality. Every sin that a man does outside the body, but he who commits sexual immorality sins against his own body. 1 Corinthians 6:18 NKJV

What is sexual immorality? It is sex outside of a marriage relationship between a man and a woman. In fact, sexual immorality is all forms of sexual sin (that includes viewing pornography). The Bible says run from it!

BAE OR NAH: FINDING THE LOVE OF YOUR LIFE

> For this is the will of God, your sanctification: that you
> should abstain from sexual immorality; that each of you
> should know how to possess his own vessel in sanctifica-
> tion and honor. 1 Thessalonians 4:3, 4 NKJV

So God is telling you here to run from sexual sin, from sex outside of marriage. Why would God tell you to run from something? Because it's dangerous, right? It's dangerous. This is a sin that will harm you physically. It's a sin that will harm you emotionally. It will break your heart. It's a sin that will harm you spiritually. It pushes you away from God. It's a sin that will harm your relationship.

If you are with someone that you think might be Bae, and you're hoping we to get married to them one day. Guess what? If you start sleeping with them, you will hurt your relationship. Even if you did end up getting married one day, you still would have hurt your relationship. Often those who will fornicate before marriage will be those who will commit adultery after marriage. If you'll cross the line before what's to keep you or them from crossing the line later on when the marriage bed isn't so hot.

A woman needs to know a man is strong enough to keep himself before she marries him so that she doesn't spend her married years wondering if he's cheating. She needs to feel secure in the fact that he can contain himself because he was able to do it with her. But if she knows he couldn't do it with her, then later on, she's going to wonder. And he needs to know that she can contain herself as well.

Temptation is everywhere. If you don't learn how to properly deal with it before you're married, then you're going to have a problem. Marriage does not fix the temptation problem. Marriage doesn't fully fix the sex problem.

There's going to be times and seasons where a man or a woman is going to be tempted by somebody else. There's going to be a time where you're going to be tempted even though you married the love of your life. So you need to learn how to overcome your flesh, as the Bible says. You need to learn to keep your body under now. If you decide to be weak then you will deal with the consequences of that.

This is why I mentioned earlier that just because a guy is big, has muscles and a deep voice doesn't mean he's a man. If he's sleeping with women he's not married to, he's weak. He's a boy in a man's body. A real man won't sleep with you before he marries you. He's trying to give you a ring. He's not playing house with you. He's making you his wife.

I saw a great post online that said "that when a real man takes you on a date, you don't have to open a car door, your purse or your legs." (By the way, real man pay for the date. If he can't pay for a date, he's not ready to date.) Violating this biblical law is why so many people end up hurt and with broken hearts in the dating world. They find that they give their body to someone who is just using them, or with whom the relationship just doesn't work out.

This sin, in particular, will wreck you emotionally. It will also wreck your life through sexually transmitted diseases, unwanted pregnancies, and more. It's just not worth it. It's better to find the person that God has for you, marry them and have sex with them without guilt or damage.

**Get Counsel**

For by wise counsel you will wage your own war, And in

a multitude of counselors there is safety. Proverbs 24:6
NKJV

You need some safety in this process. How do you get that? By listening to the people around you. We mentioned this before but I believe it bears repeating. You need to make sure that there are some people in your life that love God and love you. You need people committed to helping you recognize whether this person is God's Bae for you or not. It is not their job to tell you yes or no. It's their job to help you to realize if God is saying Yes or no. They're goal is to help you get your arms around what God's saying about your relationship.

They are asking "What does the Bible say about this? What do you have in your heart? What are you seeing in this person? Are they showing you the kind of character that the Bible says they should have it? Is this a sweet woman? Is this a strong man?"

You need to have those people in your life that can talk to you about this relationship while you are still evaluating whether or not they're Bae or not. Now that doesn't mean it has to be 80 people but there should be some people in your life that you can talk to about it who will help you get your arms around whether or not this is the person God has for you.

## Commit

There is a strange thing that happens sometimes for Christians. When they meet the person that God has for them, they get scared. All this time they had all of these options and now they have to forego all other options. The've been waiting and believing God, and finally they are here and their life is about to change. They're happy, but kind of scared too.

With anything that God is doing in your life, you may find yourself where Peter and the rest of Jesus' disciples did in Matthew 14. They were in a boat on stormy seas but they weren't there alone. Jesus was walking on the water. He told them to remain calm and then he helped Peter take a step of faith that changed his life for the better.

At some point you have to just trust God. This is everything you've been believing God for, this is everything you've been asking for. It may not have come your way the way you thought it would. The situation may not look the way that you thought it was going to look. But this is it. When you know this is it, that this is God's plan for your life, you need to commit to it.

Once you have found God's choice for you, go ahead and go after that individual. God brings you windows of opportunity in life. And when you miss those windows, they don't come back. So you want to make sure that you pursue the individual once you realize that this is God's person for you.

# CHAPTER 9: WHY AM I STILL SINGLE?

From time to time, Single Christians who want to get married approach me and ask what they are doing wrong. In essence, they are asking "why am I still single?" They are discouraged and start to feel like it is never going to happen for them or that God has forgotten them. If that's you reading this book, I want you to know that God has not forgotten about you. God hasn't forgotten about the desire of your heart.

Have you ever had to wait at a doctor's office? Although you may have had an appointment, have you ever found yourself sitting in the waiting room until the doctor is available? Maybe you had to sit in the waiting room a little bit longer than you would have liked. Maybe you approached the front desk just to make sure that they hadn't forgotten about you or to inform them that you had an appointment. If so, my guess is that they told you that you were not forgotten. They probably told you that they were just running behind that day and asked you to hang in there a little longer. Ever experienced that? How do you respond to that? You have a choice. You can make a big deal out of it and leave the doctor's office without the care that you need or you can calm down, take a seat and be patient.

Well, you may be sitting in the marriage waiting room right now!

You're waiting to meet the person that God has for you. And you might be saying, "Hey God, remember me? My friend just got married and they had a baby. And I'm still single! God, have you forgotten about the desire of my heart?" If so, let me remind you that you have an appointment! There is a date on God's calendar when you will meet Bae. Continue to believe God, be patient, and make sure that you're in position to receive them.

In this chapter, we're going to talk about four reasons that may explain why you're still single. The first is that there are some adjustments that you need to make before you are ready for God to send you Bae. In short, you may still be single because you're not ready.

## Reason #1: You're Not Ready

The horse is prepared for the day of battle, But deliverance is of the Lord. Proverbs 21:31 NKJV

"Pastor, what on earth does this scripture have to do with what we're talking about?" you may ask. Well, notice just how God works. Of course, he's talking to a people that live in a time where when they went to war they would do it on horseback. They would have swords and shields and the like. He's talking about the fact that before you would go into battle, you would take the time to make sure your horse was prepared. So obviously, you would feed the horse, you would shoe the horse, you would saddle horse etc. Before you went on the battlefield, you would do your part.

But of course, the people of God went into battle believing that, ultimately, God is the one who would give them victory. They believed that whether or not they actually survived, whether or not they actually defeated their enemies was dependent on God doing something supernatural on the battlefield. Although that was true, although God is the one that would ultimately bring them victory, they still had a part to play. They still had to prepare the horse.

That is true when it comes to working with God in this area as well. God has a part to play but you have a part to play as well. There is a man-ward side and a God-ward side to every blessing from God. Even though you meeting Bae will ultimately be supernatural, you still have a part to play.

And so having said that, let me ask you a question. Are you praying for what you're not prepared for? Maybe you feel like you're waiting on God and God is actually waiting on you! You may need to ask yourself "Am I really ready for God to bring Bae to me?"

Let me give you a few things to look at to help you evaluate yourself so that you are actually ready for Bae. This list may sound familiar, because this is actually what we said you're looking for in Bae. You need to prepare by...

**Developing the Habits of a Christian**
That means you need to spend daily time with God in the Bible and in prayer. You need to go to church consistently. You need to find a way to serve because you don't go to church just for you, you go to help other people. So you need to be the kind of person that thinks like that. Most importantly, you need to be somebody that's actually making a mark in this world through serving and sharing Jesus.

**Having the Fruit of the Spirit evident in your Life**
You need to be somebody that's walking in love, joy, peace and gentleness. You need to have a servant's heart. We talked in a previous chapter about being a sweet woman or a strong man. You want to develop that kind of character.

## Living Pure

That means you're not having sex before marriage. If you're having sex before marriage right now, God is not bringing Bae to you. He will not bless mess. Plus, you're not ready for them yet. You need to be free of vices such as drinking, smoking, gambling, looking at porn etc. You need to learn how to control your mouth. God's not bringing you Bae so that you can cuss him or her out!

## Discovering your Assignment and Pursuing It

In other words, you have figured out what God has called you to do and you're actually chasing after that. You are totally dedicated to God's plan for your life, not just your plan for your life.

## Being a Good Steward over your Money, Body & Home

You're somebody who has developed the financial habits that are necessary for you to be financially healthy. That means that you're not overspending. You have a budget and you live within that budget. You act your wage. You're somebody that's taking care of your body.

The issue of being a good steward over your body is kind of a touchy subject. This is because some people feel like I'm saying that you've got to be a size two or you need to have muscles like the Rock. I'm not saying that, but I am saying that you need to do the best that you can with the body that God has given you. That's what you expect of your Bae, right? You don't want them to show up all sloppy, right? You want Bae to look good! Well, you ought to do the same thing.

You ought to do what it takes so that you look your best. And let's be honest. Muscles matter to some women, shape matters to some men. So these things are actually important because they're important to you. So why wouldn't they be important to Bae?

Are you somebody that's properly stewarding the body God has given you by working out, getting in shape and looking your very best? Of course, you should be a good steward over your home. It shouldn't be a mess (neither should your car!).

You see, when you take care of your business then you are ready for Bae. Then you're in position for God to bring that person to you. Andy Stanley says it this way "Are you the person you're looking for is looking for?" That's a great quote isn't it? So, are you? Are you the person that Bae is looking for? You have a list of what you want in Bae but you need to *be* the List for Bae.

I ran across a great post online by a man named Brian Bullock. He posted some signs that you're not ready to be married. This is a little bit more practical than what we've been talking about, but it will get you thinking!

**8 Signs You're Not Ready to Be Married:**

1. If having to check in with somebody bothers you, then you're not ready to be married.

2. If having to talk about your thoughts and feelings gets on your nerves, then you're not ready to be married.

3. If dirty clothes, hair in the sink, and loud snoring make you cringe,then you're not ready to be married.

4. If having one bank account makes you feel like you're in prison, then you're not ready to be married.

5. If saying "I'm sorry," asking for forgivenss and apologiing often makes you feel like less of a person, then you're not ready to be married.

6. If the thought of having sex with the same person 2-3 times a week makes you wanna throw up, then you're not ready to be married.

7. If the idea of making someone a sandwich makes you feel like a slave, then you're not ready to be married.

8. If spending less time with your family and friends so you can spend more time with your spouse bothers you, then you're not ready to be married.

You need to take a moment and evaluate yourself. If you're saying, "I want Bae" but you haven't gotten yourself together yet, you're not ready for Bae. If you haven't developed the habits that we've talked about, if you haven't developed your character, if you haven't gotten some stuff out of your life that shouldn't be there, if you haven't gotten your money or body together. You're not ready yet! Not for God's Bae for you.

I'm sure you could find a Bae but not the Bae that you really want. And that's okay. That's one reason why you're reading this book. I'm here to help you get ready. The bottom line is that if you want God's Bae for you, you're going to have to start working on these things and allow God to help you to get to the place where you are the list, where you are the person that Bae is looking for.

**Reason #2: You're Too Picky**
Could it be that you're still single because you're too picky? Stay with me because I don't mean this in the way that you're thinking. Let's go back to Genesis 24 and pull out some more truth that will help us.

> For the Lord, the God of heaven, who took me from my father's house and my native land, solemnly promised to give this land to my descendants. He will send his angel

ahead of you, and he will see to it that you find a wife there
for my son. Genesis 24:12

Notice once again that there's a matchmaking angel! One of the
things that angels do is bring people together so that they can get
married! They help bring people together that God wants to be
together. This is a supernatural process! Heaven is writing your
love story!

Clearly, God had somebody in mind for Isaac and so he was sending the angel ahead of Abraham's servant. He was sending his
angel to ensure that he met Rebekah, the person God had in mind
for Isaac.

God has somebody in mind for you! He may have his angel working on them right now too!

> "O LORD, God of my master, Abraham," he prayed. "Please
> give me success today, and show unfailing love (favor) to
> my master, Abraham. See, I am standing here beside this
> spring, and the young women of the town are coming out
> to draw water. This is my request. I will ask one of them,
> 'Please give me a drink from your jug.' If she says, 'Yes,
> have a drink, and I will water your camels, too!'—let her be
> the one you have selected as Isaac's wife. This is how I will
> know that you have shown unfailing love to my master."
> Genesis 24:13, 14 NLT

God had already selected someone to be Isaac's wife. Now it was
not that she didn't have free will. If we were to read the rest of the
story we would find out that she still has a choice on whether or
not she's going to follow God's plan for her life or not. But God had
selected someone. So let's go back to my point. If you're asking
"why am I still single?" It may be because you're too picky. What I
mean by that is you actually think you get to choose your spouse.
God has brought to you the person he has for you and you're so

picky that you're actually rejecting God's choice for you.

In the book of Esther, we read about Esther being selected to be the queen out of a huge pool of women. And when disaster struck her uncle came to her.

> If you keep quiet at a time like this, deliverance and relief for the Jews will arise from some other place, but you and your relatives will die. Who knows if perhaps you were made queen for just such a time as this?" Esther 4:14 NLT

God actually is the one that selected Esther to marry that King. God said, "this is my plan for you." Why? God needed her in that position to save his people. God has selected you to be with someone as well because he has some things he wants you to accomplish together. You are his power couple, you've got some work to do. So you need to take a step back and decide whether or not you're going to go with God's choice for you or your choice for you.

You've got to make a decision today on whether or not you're going pick your spouse, or you're going to say, "God, I trust you. Whoever you pick that's who I'm going to be with." That can be tough to do in any area of your life. It's tough to just throw away whatever your plans were for your career and say, "God, I'll take on whatever career you have for me." It's tough when you want to live somewhere that's warm and God says, "I'm going put you in cold Detroit?" Right? It's tough when you say "I would love to be in a little tiny church" and God says, "I want you to be in this massive church." It's tough to give God your life, but you're supposed to give him your life. And that includes your spouse. You got to allow him to choose the person he has for you because he knows what's best for you. He knows the person who you'll be happy with, and it's the one he has selected for you!

You know, I've talked to a number of people about their love stories, people that have have learned by experience that God's choice is the best choice. They thought that the person they were going to marry would look or be one way and they are another, but it turns out that God knew them better than they knew themselves.

And I'm here to tell you, God knows *you* better than you know yourself! God also knows what that person's going to be like seven years from now, 15 years from now, 30 years from now, he knows how that person will respond when tragedy strikes. He knows how that person will flow with you in raising your kids. He knows things you don't know. He sees the end from the beginning.

So you've got to make a decision to roll with God's choice, not just with your choice. You've got to decide to recognize that there are things that are more important than even how somebody happens to look right now, or whether or not their bicep has an extra inch or not. That's important, but what's more important is the character of the individual, what's more important is that your calling's match, what's more important is that this is the person God has for you.

You want to see something really deep about this story? Look at Rebekah's side of it. Here's a young woman who was just going to get water for her family. She woke up that day not knowing that that day she was going to get connected to the servant of her rich husband to be. (You never know what God will do in 24 hours! Don't get too discouraged if you don't see something right now, because you can get a phone call and it could change your life!)

So, she's just getting water, probably like she did every day. And here this man comes. He asked for some water and because she's already a sweetheart, she gives him water and gives water to his camels. Then he starts to tell her where he's from and why he's there. He's there to take her to his master in another country. A man she's never met and that she's supposed to marry. Talk about Married at First Sight!

At least she can see that he has some money due to the camels that the servant brought, but she doesn't know this man. She doesn't know what he looks like. She's never been to where he's living. I mean, this is a huge, huge life altering moment. And yet, when she was asked, "will you go?" She said, "I will go." Why? Because she heard this man's testimony and she and her family had also come to the conclusion that this was God's plan for her. She trusted God enough to say, "even if I don't know the man, even if I don't know where I'm going, I know that if you have done this is, it is for my good."

Thank God today that you get to meet the person you're going to marry before you do. You get to date them. So things work differently today then they did then but we still ultimately have to come to the same conclusion as she did. You got to get to the place where you decide that you're going to trust God when it comes to your spouse and not just yourself.

## Reason #3: You're Messing with a Counterfeit

What's a counterfeit? According to Oxford Dictionary, a counterfeit is a fraudulent imitation of something else. It seems, at times, that Satan likes to send counterfeits to God's people to prevent them from marrying God's choice for them.

Let's look again at the story of Jacob and Laban. Remember that Jacob was so in love with Rachel that he decided that he would serve Laban seven years for the privilege of marrying her. Well, seven years had come and gone and Jacob was finally going to get to marry her, or so he thought.

Finally, the time came for him to marry her. "I have fulfilled my agreement," Jacob said to Laban. "Now give me my wife so I can sleep with her." So Laban invited everyone in the neighborhood and prepared a wedding feast. But that night, when it was dark, Laban took Leah to Jacob, and he slept with her. (Laban had given Leah a servant, Zilpah, to be her maid.) But when Jacob woke up in the morning—it was Leah! "What have you done to me?" Jacob raged at Laban. "I worked seven years for Rachel! Why have you tricked me?" Genesis 29:21-25 NLT

This is so wrong! Jacob ended up sleeping with Rachel thinking it was Leah (there were no light bulbs then)! He wakes up the next morning and goes, "Whoa, this isn't Rachel." And what's wild is that Leah went along with it. Most likely, she was forced to. That's another story. My point in bringing this up is that too many people are messing with Leah instead of Rachel. Too many are messing with Bozo instead of Boaz.

I had the opportunity to go to South Korea a number of years ago. I noticed when shopping there that many of the stores there had purses that looked very similar to what you would see in some of our more expensive stores here. Upon closer inspection it became very clear that although they looked the part they were not the same as the designer purses that we're used to seeing in our country. They were knock-offs. Are you dating a knock-off? Do you think your man is an LV (Louis Vuitton) and he's Crazy! You thought your woman was an Apple phone and she's actually a Pear phone!

I'm just joking around but my point is that sometimes because we're impatient and needy, we settle for someone that is not God choice for us. Some of us have waited years for Rachel. And yet, at the end we give in and marry Leah, and then we wonder five,ten, fifteen or twenty years later, "why is my marriage so bad?" It's because you decided to marry the counterfeit instead of waiting for the real thing.

An additional problem with continuing to date the wrong person is that they're actually blocking you from getting the person God has for you.

You see, God's timing is precise. In first Kings 17, we'd read about a time of famine. And God told the man to go by the brook Cedron. God said, "I'll have Ravens feed you there and you'll drink of that brook." When the man of God (Elijah) arrived at the brook the ravens were there with the food and the bread every day. Eventually God said, "I want you to leave this brook. And I want you to go to this town called Zarephath. And when you get to this town, there's a widow woman there that I've already commanded to sustain you." So he obeyed God and when he arrived at the gate, she was there! God's timing was perfect. She needed a miracle and he showed up right when she needed it the most!

Notice how God timed that. Well, this principle is true when it comes to you being with the person that God has for you. God has in mind and time when you all are going to meet. He has already planned out your love story. However, it's hard for him to make it happen when you're dating Leah or Bozo right now.

This is one reason why I mentioned in the last chapter that when you know that the person you are presently dating is not God's person for you that you need to end the relationship as soon as possible. It may not be easy. Obviously, your emotions are involved. You may have family and friends that may be critical of your decision. But when you know that you know that this isn't it, end the relationship. Do it first of all for their sake but also for yours because you need to be in position to receive God's Bae for you. And you're not going to be in position while you're messing around with the counterfeit. Timing matters with supernatural things. So stop playing around and get in position to receive God's best for you.

Let me add to this real quickly that some are still caught up and chasing almost or has been relationships and so they're missing out on the phenomenal relationship that God has prepared for them. You're chasing somebody that hasn't even really committed to you. You're still dreaming about a future with somebody that you haven't even been on a date with or you're chasing after an ex, trying to rekindle something. There's a reason why they haven't committed to you. There's a reason why they're an ex. Let it go and let God bring you his Bae for you.

### Reason #4: It's Not Time Yet

Here's another reason why you may still be Single. It's not time yet. We just finished talking about how timing matters with supernatural things. Here's an example in John 17.

> After saying all these things, Jesus looked up to heaven and said, "Father, the hour has come. Glorify your Son so he can give glory back to you. John 17:1 NLT

Jesus is talking about the hour of his death and resurrection. He's actually talking about what time it was on God's clock. There was a time when this was supposed to happen and he knew in his heart it was now time.

Jesus knew it was the right time because he has the Holy Spirit in him to guide him. He *knew* when it was his season and you can do the same thing when it comes to dating and marriage. You can know when it's just not your time to date and you can also know when God is saying that it's time.

> To everything there is a season, A time for every purpose under heaven; Ecclesiastes 3:1 NKJV

God has a perfect season and a perfect time for you to meet Bae and it may not be when you think it should be. For example, remember the story of Isaac and Rebekah that we've been studying. Isaac was 40 when that happened. Why did God wait that long? I don't know. I do know that God timed it in such a way that when his mother died and he was hurting over it, Rebekah came into his life and he was comforted.

Maybe that's why he did it. Be careful of saying, "Oh God, I thought I'd be married by 25 or 30 and here I am 45 years old. I'm never going to get married!" Don't put a deadline on God. Trust God and be led by the Holy Spirit that he has placed in your heart to guide you.

The Bible teaches us how God leads us. First of all, God leads us by what we find in the Bible. This book has given you a number of scriptures that you can use to evaluate whether you are ready or not. God also leads us by our spirit, through the Holy Spirit in our hearts. The Holy Spirit communicates with us through an inward witness, God's nudges. Sometimes he does through an inward voice, God's whispers. Sometimes through the voice of the Holy Spirit, God's bullhorn. Sometimes through visions and dreams, God's Facetime. By the way, anytime He leads you through your spirit, what he is saying is not going to contradict what the Bible says instead it's going to agree with what's in the Bible.

The key is to make sure that you're checking in with God to make sure that you're operating in his timing. If you're not in the season to date yet don't fret or get upset. It doesn't mean it's not going to happen. It means you need to focus on preparing. It means there's probably some adjustments that you need to make. There are probably some things you need to do so that you are ready for God's Bae for you. And let me tell you when it happens in God's timing, you can fully enjoy it! God's love story for you is the best story for you and your Bae.

So we've covered a number of reasons why you may still be single. But what if you're actually ready right now? What does the Bible has to say to you? But what if I am ready? Here's a great scripture for you.

> Hope deferred makes the heart sick, But when the desire comes, it is a tree of life. Prov. 13:12 NKJV

God makes dreams come to pass. Notice that this scripture didn't say *if* the desire comes. It says *when* it comes! The day comes when desire comes!

> A desire accomplished is sweet to the soul. Prov. 13:19a NKJV

God is a God who will cause your dreams to come to pass one day. When he does, you're going to do what they did in Psalm 126. The Bible says that the people of God felt like they were dreaming. They were singing and laughing. They even heard other people who didn't know God personally say that God had done great things for them.

One day, you're going to have that experience. You're going to wake up and it's going to be your wedding day. And your family and friends will be gathered together to celebrate with you. You'll stand next to the person that you asked God for, the person that you dreamed of, in front of a minister. They will be so in love you with and you with them. You will both love God together and be excited about the bright future ahead of you together.

You'll have your reception and you'll try to dance or you're actually dance (if you're like me it will definitely be a *try!*). You'll have your wedding night followed by a wonderful honeymoon in some beautiful place. One day, you'll say "I'm so glad I waited for God's Bae for me!" because together you'll be a power couple that's enjoying life and making a Mark in this world for God. I challenge you to hang on to that.

# CHAPTER 10: KEYS TO DISCOVERING BAE

L et me give you some keys to discovering Bae. Just a couple of things you can do to make sure that you get God's Bae for you:

**Make a List and Check it Twice**

The Bible says in Habakkuk 2, *"write the vision and make it plain."* You need to sit down and write out what exactly you are looking for in Bae. We've already went through some things in this series to give you an idea of what you should be looking for, but there may be some other things you want to add to that. Once you've written your list, use it to evaluate whether or not you're going to even pursue a relationship with different individuals that happen to approach you (women), or that you happen to be interested in approaching (men).

**Get in Position to Meet Them**

In Genesis 24, Abraham's servant went to the well, where the women would normally come out. He was in a place where he could actually meet somebody that Isaac could marry. If you want a Christian woman or a Christian man. You probably need to go to church. That's a good start, right? You need to get out and get around people.

Nowadays we have social media and dating apps. I know that sometimes Christians wonder, if we should be on those or use those to find Bae (or for Bae to find us). I personally don't have a problem with using social media or dating apps that are appropriate. Obviously, there's always bad versions of everything, but I believe that even as a woman, it is appropriate to present yourself on a website or dating app. I don't think you should be sending unsolicited messages to men that you are attracted to. Let them make the first move.

However, my opinion is that it is appropriate to present yourself there because that's how people meet today. Ultimately, you need to be led by God in regards to whether you should go that route or not.

## Date with Integrity

Don't play games with people's emotions. Remember, Love wouldn't lead people on. Love also wouldn't have sex with someone before you marry them.

## Take Your Time

The Bible says in 1 Thessalonians 5, to prove all things. That means to put all spiritual things to the test. You're not going to figure out everything that you need to know about that person and you're not going to do everything you need to do as a couple in a month. Take the time necessary to be sure this is God's choice for you. Take the time to listen to family and friends and make sure you're making the right choice which flows into my next point.

## Listen to Godly Counsel

Make sure that you talk to family and friends about your relationship. Your goal is not for them to tell you what to do but for them to help you realize what God is saying about the relationship.

## Be Led by God's Peace

As we said a few moments ago, God will lead you by his inward peace. And so when you have peace about a relationship, keep on following that. If you've got a "check" in your heart that seems to make you feel like something is not right, pay attention to that, get before God and let him tell you what that is. Once you have peace, follow that peace all the way up to the altar. Follow peace all the way into your happily ever after with God's Bae for you.

You may be saying, "why am I still single?" But if you'll make the adjustments that we've talked about in the last chapter, you won't be single for long!

# CHAPTER 11: SINGLE AGAIN

L ife can be messy.

Sometimes things happen that we did not plan for or anticipate. For example, you marry the person who you believe is the love of your life and, somehow, your once fairy tale relationship ends in divorce. Even worse, you have a wonderful marriage to a wonderful person and then they pass away. Now you find yourself single again. You want to remarry one day but that requires you going back out into the dating world again. Except this time, the world is different. This time dating is different. This time you're different.

How do you navigate in this new world that you find yourself in? How do you move on from your past? How do you get past the idea that you're used goods or leftovers now? Does God still have a Bae for you? If you want to remarry and want to know the answer to these questions then this chapter is for you! Let's start by seeing what the Bible has to say about your situation.

**Know What The Bible Says About Your Situation**

In first Corinthians 7, we find Paul answering questions about relationships. He's talking to people who are unmarried. He's telling him God's perspective concerning their status, and whether or not they should get married. Then he begins to address people who are married.

> But if the husband or wife who isn't a believer insists on leaving, let them go. In such cases the believing husband or wife is no longer bound to the other... 1 Corinthians 7:15 NLT

He's talking to believers here, and he's talking about a situation where a believer is married to someone that is an unbeliever (by the way, in Matthew 18:15-17 Jesus says that a believer who chooses to resist counsel from multiple sources is to be treated like an unbeliever as well). He's talking about this person who has an unbelieving spouse who does not want to be married to him anymore. He's saying that in those kinds of situations, let them go. Notice that he uses the terminology "in such cases." In other words, this is a certain type of circumstance. He's saying that the believing husband or wife is no longer bound to that individual. In other words, God considers them free of that marriage relationship. They're no longer in covenant.

> ...for God has called you to live in peace. 1 Corinthians 7:15 NLT

Notice God's heart here. That word peace means quietness and rest. He doesn't want you living in the middle of a home where there is a war going on between you and your spouse because they don't want to serve God and they don't want to be with you anymore.

So we can see a couple of things here about marriage and even divorce. We can see that God acknowledges divorce, whether he's pleased with it or not. That's something you can see throughout the Bible (see Jesus with the women by the well. He acknowledged her 5 previous marriages). You can see that God has given every person free will. God will allow people to choose to go the wrong direction in life. He will honor that choice. A clear example is Adam and Eve in the garden of Eden, they had everything and yet they chose to partake of the fruit that changed the direction of their lives.

Not only can people make that kind of choice but we know that people do it all the time. People that don't know God and people that do know God (but choose to backslide from his plan for their life) sometimes make a decision to go a different direction in their lives. When they do, God doesn't hold the other person accountable for their decisions.

The fact is that sometimes life just isn't fair. You could be a good spouse, someone that isn't perfect but surely hasn't done anything worthy of the marriage being ended, and you're spouse could still choose to cheat on you. You could have a spouse that chooses to backslide on God and thus choose to leave you because you want to continue to serve God. You could do everything pretty well and still have somebody turn around and betray you.

You may say, "Well, I don't know about that, pastor. If a person is divorced they must've done something wrong." In any long-term relationship both parties have done some things wrong. I don't care who you have a relationship with. That's not just true in a marriage relationship.

Everybody's going to make a mistake from time to time. However, not every mistake rises to the place where they are grounds for cheating, abandonment and, ultimately, divorce, right? So sure, people will make mistakes in marriage relationships (so will you) and sometimes people may look back on their previous marriage and say, "I wish I did this or that differently." However, that doesn't mean that their former spouse were right to do what they did.

Think about this, Jesus was perfect. He was a perfect man. He was a perfect minister when he walked on the earth and Judas still betrayed him. Jesus did everything right and Judas left him. And it wasn't just Judas, there were others that left him as well! Once again, Adam and Eve were in the perfect situation, they were in the perfect will of God and yet Eve allowed the serpent to deceive her and still chose to eat the fruit of the knowledge of good and evil! Adam wasn't deceived and yet he chose being with Eve over staying in God's plan for his life!

My point is that you can find yourself in a situation where you are divorced and it not necessarily be because you did something that was worthy of divorce. It can simply be because the other person chose to go another direction in their life. So Paul's acknowledging that.

A key thing that we can see from this opening of scripture is that Paul is applying the law of love to different relationship situations including divorce. Sometimes, when you talk about this issue, people say, "well, Jesus said in Matthew 19 that the only grounds for divorce is when the other person has committed sexual sin, when they committed adultery."

Well, yes, Jesus said that. But Jesus was talking to people that lived under the Old Testament law. He was properly interpreting what the law said about marriage. But, of course, if you're a Christian today you don't live under the law. As a Christian, you now live under grace. The only law that we follow is the law of love.

What Paul was doing throughout first Corinthians 7, was interpreting these situations, including marriage and divorce, from the context of the law of love. And the law of love says that God's not going to require you to stay in a situation where your un-believing or backslidden spouse has decided that they no longer want to be married to you.

> If we confess our sins, he is faithful and just to forgive us, our sins and to cleanse us from all unrighteousness. 1 John 1:9 KJV

Now there are cases where people have gotten a divorce and it is their fault. They messed up. They blew it. What do you do when you've made such an error? (Notice that the Bible is talking to believers here in 1 John 1. John starts the book off my saying "my little children" and says if *we* confess our sins including himself in it).

If we confess our sins who are we confessing it to? To God. The good news is that God is faithful. You can count on him. He is also just meaning that because Jesus already paid for your sin, he has the legal right to forgive you and cleanse you from all of our sins. So if you messed up and it's your fault, go before God ask him for forgiveness. God will forgive you and cleanse you.

> He who covers his sins will not prosper, but whoever con-fesses and forsakes them will have mercy. Proverbs 28:13 NKJV

If God says, "you're forgiven." If God says, as he does in Isaiah 43, "I remember your sins no more" then you can rest assured that you are forgiven, cleansed and that God remembers our sin no more! Divorce, even when it is your fault, is not the unpardonable sin. Treating it like it is, is not biblical. God's word is very clear that even if you messed up and blown up your life in some way or another, God is a God who will forgive you and cleanse you.

Let's see what else Paul says about this:

> Now concerning virgins: I have no commandment from the Lord; yet I give judgment as one whom the Lord in His mercy has made trustworthy. I suppose therefore that this is good because of the present distress--that it is good for a man to remain as he is: Are you bound to a wife? Do not seek to be loosed. Are you loosed from a wife? Do not seek a wife. But even if you do marry, you have not sinned (MSG - certainly no sin in getting married, whether you're a virgin or not); and if a virgin marries, she has not sinned. Nevertheless such will have trouble in the flesh, but I would spare you. 1 Corinthians 7:25-28 NKJV

Paul is referring to a season that they were in, a season of great persecution. He once again makes the point that its better to be single (a theme of his in this chapter). However, he mentions that if you're loosed from a wife it is not a sin to marry again. The Message translation says "certainly no sin in getting married whether you're a virgin (talking about somebody that's only been single) or not."

Are there "such cases" or situations where it is appropriate for someone who was divorced to remarry? Absolutely. I encourage you to get ahold of Kenneth Hagin's book 'Marriage, Divorce, and Remarriage' if you have additional questions about this. Also, it would be beneficial to talk to your spiritual leadership, and most importantly, talk to God to ensure that you are 100% clear on what God says about your situation.

For the rest of this chapter, I'm going to talk directly to those for whom remarriage is a godly option including those who are widowed, and desire to re-marry.  If you're a widow, unfortunately, your previous relationship ended in tragedy. God still has a future for you. He can comfort and restore you. If you're divorced and yet you're saying I still want to get married, that you want God's Bae for you, God wants you to have that too! He's not decided that you're done, that your life is over, that you are now somehow put in the used basket or are somehow worthless.

In the Bible, you can find that many men and women of God who God did great things through, had a past:

Adam fell.

Noah got drunk.

Abraham lied.

Jacob cheated.

Moses murdered.

Rahab prostituted.

David fornicated.

Jonah fled.

Thomas doubted.

Peter denied.

Paul persecuted.

The first person that saw Jesus raised from the dead was Mary

Magdalene, a woman who had been possessed with seven demon spirits. Can you imagine the things that she did? Yet, she was the first (and will always be the first) to see the resurrected Jesus. You see, we are all an ex-something and God still has a future for all of us, just like he did for them.

There does seems to be a stigma that comes with divorce especially among Christians. That may be tough to deal with at times. I think the answer to that emotional challenge is found by simply looking to the cross. Jesus allowed himself to be placed on a cross for you. He was stripped naked, labeled as a the worst of criminals and ridiculed. He was in a shameful position, right? One of the main goals of putting someone on a cross is to shame them. The Bible says that he was there not because of his sin, but for our sin.

> He, for the joy (of obtaining the prize) that was set before endured the cross, despising and ignoring the shame, and is now seated at the right hand of the throne of God. Hebrews 12:2b AMPC

While he was on the cross Jesus disregarded and ignored the shame. He refused to take the shame on him. Instead of somebody saying "shame on you' and him accepting that, he thought "no shame off of me!" That's what you need to do. Whether your marriage ended because your former spouse did wrong by you or the relationship ended because you messed up and had to repent to God, you must choose to live shame-free. What happened is, ultimately, between you and God. It has nothing to do with anyone else. It has nothing to do with their opinion or perspective.

One of the things that I've learned is that people make judgments about things they know nothing about. They don't know that your spouse may have cheated on you. They don't know that your spouse decided to walk away from God and you. They don't know.

They don't know that you fully repented before God. So it's just not their business! Refuse to accept the shame. It doesn't matter what they think. If they have a problem with you dating a re-marrying so what? What matters is that you're right with God, that you're listening to godly counsel, and following God's plan for your life.

# CHAPTER 12: LET GOD HEAL YOU

In Acts 9, we find the churches of God coming out of a season of great persecution. Christians were arrested. Christians were killed for their faith. The apostle Paul (at that time the Bible called him Saul) was one of the main guys doing this, but God stopped the persecution mainly by helping him to become a Christian!

> Then the churches throughout all Judea Galilee, and Samaria had peace and were edified and walking in the fear of the Lord and in the comfort of the Holy Spirit, were multiplied. Acts 9:31 KJV

Notice that God edified the churches, meaning that he built them up spiritually. He helped them to live holy (if you are walking in the fear of the Lord, you're going to live Holy before him). He comforted them, meaning that he healed them emotionally (God cares about how you feel!). Then they multiplied. There was a significant move of God. Those churches saw many people come to God as result of what God was doing. They enjoyed seeing the results that they and God wanted. (Never forget that God does not plant churches to take care of Christians. He plants churches to reach people far from God. The goal is to bring people into the family of God.)

Check out the order that this happened in. Sometimes what we want to do is jump into multiplication. To apply this principle to what we're talking about in this book, we want to jump into God bringing Bae into our lives. We want God to bring them without having allowed God to heal us from the damage of what we previously experienced.

A church has to be taught the word of God before it can multiply. Most Christians get that. That's important. It's important for people to live Holy so that God's anointing (power) works. That is a must before the church can multiply. Most Christians get that too. But what jumped out at me one day as I was studying this, is that they needed to be comforted first before they were ready to reach the amount of people that God wanted them to reach. They need to be healed emotionally. They needed to allow God to heal their hearts.

The same thing is true for us. When you come out of a traumatic season in your life, you need to let God heal you. You need to be healed before you talk about moving into a new season. I like something that Shaun Nepstad said, "It's so important to be healed or you'll live broken and break things." That's so true! So many people come out of seasons like this, and instead of being healed and then going on into a new season, they take that pain into a new relationship and they create issues in that relationship and end up even more broken (not to mention hurting the other individual).

Healing comes before progress. Healing comes before a move of God in your life including in the area of relationships. The good news is that God can completely heal your heart.

The Spirit of the Lord is upon Me, because He has anointed Me to preach the gospel to the poor; He has sent me to heal the brokenhearted... Luke 4:18a NKJV

All praise to God, the Father of our Lord Jesus Christ. God is our merciful Father and the source of all comfort. He comforts us in all our troubles so that we can comfort others. When they are troubled, we will be able to give them the same comfort God has given us. 2 Corinthians 1:3, 4 NLT

For He bruises, but He binds up; He wounds, but His hands make whole. Job 5:18 NKJV

God can make your heart whole again. God can cause you to be completely healed of what you just went through. God can cause you to get to a place where you don't even have a scar on your heart. He can get you to the place where this no longer has an impact on your emotional life. Now for that to happen, you've got to make the decision to come out of the cave.

**Come Out of The Cave**

In 1 Kings 19, Elijah, the prophet of God had quite the pity party! God had just done something great through him. He called down fire from heaven! But in the beginning of chapter 19, we find out that queen Jezebel has put a price on his head. So he's running for his life.

Finally, he finds himself under a Juniper tree and telling God to kill him. Eventually God tells him to go Mount Horeb and when arrives he he sits in a cave while waiting for God to talk to him.

Sometimes when we go through really difficult seasons in our lives, we go sit in an emotional cave and, if we're not careful, we stay there permanently.

> So Tamar remained desolate in her brother Absalom's house. 2 Samuel 13:20 KJV

Tamar's story in the Bible is tragic. She was raped by her own brother and, of course, it devastated her for many reasons. What made the story even more tragic is where it left her. The last thing we read about her is that she remained desolate. The word desolate here means stunned, devastated and destroyed. She didn't just end up in this horrible emotional state. She stayed there. You can't stay there.

Sometimes you find yourself in a valley. Sometimes horrible things happen to you.

> I also saw other things in this life that were not fair. The fastest runner does not always win the race; the strongest soldier does not always win the battle; wise people don't always get the food; smart people don't always get the wealth; educated people don't always get the praise they deserve. When the time comes, bad things can happen to anyone! Ecclesiastes 9:11 ERV

Sometimes bad things happen to good people. Sometimes it's because good people have opened the door to those bad things happening. Other times your situation could simply be the result of living in a world where you have an enemy who is constantly attacking you. Satan hates you. He's going to do everything he can to destroy you. And so when you're in those situations, when you're going through those types of things, yeah, you might find yourself in a cave upset and broken. However, you can't stay there. You just can't.

David was in a situation where he made a mistake and it led to the people he cared about losing their loved ones. The Bible says in 1 Samuel 30 that his own men, whom he loved, were thinking about stoning him. Also, he had lost his family. So, he was depressed. And yet what did he do? He made a decision to seek God. The Bible says he encouraged himself in the Lord his God.

He decided to come out of the cave. He decided to do whatever it took to get out of his emotional state. He decided to start to thank, praise, worship God and pray before God until God was able to give him the strength to break out of that emotional cave and to step into the wisdom that God had for him. That wisdom led to him and his men getting back everything that they lost.

You must come out of the cave. The way you're going to do that is by doing what David did, by pressing into God. Open your Bible again and read the scripture. Thank God for what he's done in your life. Praise and worship him. Pray in your understanding. Pray in the spirit. You might need to go to a conference or read a book. You may need to take a couple of days and just do these things only. You've got to press into God and allow God to heal you. If you'll let God heal your heart, eventually you'll be in position for God to bring you your new Bae.

**Learn from Past Relationships**

"Pastor, you just finished talking about healing from it. I don't want to think about it anymore that makes it harder to heal!" I'm not telling you to dwell on it because if you think too much about what's happened, it'll cause you to get down emotionally. However, you do still need to learn from your past, including a past relationship.

A wise man will hear and increase learning, And a man of understanding will attain wise counsel. Proverbs 1:5 NKJV

You want to be the wise man. If you look in the book of Proverbs, you'll see, it says a lot about the wise man. The wise man has success in every area of his life, that would include in relationships. The Bible says that wisdom is a tree of life to you meaning that if you'll partake of the wisdom of God (like Eve did of the tree of the knowledge of good and evil) it'll bring God's life into every area of your life.

Wise man hear God's word whether it's written or spoken directly into their heart. They hear godly counsel from other people. That's what we see at the end of the scripture. They attain to wise counsel. A wise man won't shut their ears. They won't decide to not to hear anything from God or anyone else about this area of their life. That's what the fool does. The fool says that he didn't do nothing wrong and doesn't need to learning anything. The wise man says, "Let me hear what God is saying. Let me learn so that I can make some adjustments."

Give instruction to a wise man and he will be yet wiser: teach a just man, and he will increase in learning. Proverbs 9:9 KJV

We should always be increasing our knowledge base. One of the ways that we do that is by looking back at our lives and seeing where maybe we should've done some things differently. Our goal is to learn from those moments and make the necessary adjustments in our lives so that we can have better outcomes.

> Jesus knew what they were saying, so he said, "Why are you arguing about having no bread? Don't you know or understand even yet? Are your hearts too hard to take it in? 'You have eyes—can't you see? You have ears—can't you hear?' Don't you remember anything at all? When I fed the 5,000 with five loaves of bread, how many baskets of leftovers did you pick up afterward?" "Twelve," they said. "And when I fed the 4,000 with seven loaves, how many large baskets of leftovers did you pick up?" "Seven," they said. "Don't you understand yet?" he asked them. Mark 8:17-21 NLT

I think sometimes God looks at us and says, "don't you understand? You still don't get it?" In Hebrews 5, he says, "by now you ought to be teachers." There does come a point where you should learn from the past!

The goal is to learn and to grow. Whether your previous relationship was great or not, whether it ending was your fault or not. There's always something to learn from it. There's always room for improvement. You want to take what you've learned into your relationship with God's Bae for you.

There's a movie I really liked called Groundhog Day. It's probably about 20 years old now. Bill Murray was the star of it. If you haven't seen it, I'm going to ruin it for you but you had 20 years to watch it! It starts with his character eally being a jerk. He goes to this small town and he's got to cover Groundhog day as a reporter. One of his colleagues is a beautiful woman that he really likes. But of course, since he's a jerk, she sees him as a jerk. He has no chance of winning her.

He finds that when he wakes up the next day, he's been sentenced to living Groundhog day over and over again. So throughout the movie, he goes through so many changes. He even attempts to end his life. Eventually, his attitude changes about the situation he finds himself in and he decides to improve himself. He learns how to play a piano. He learns how to treat people. He learns how to properly engage with this woman, how to treat her. It's not until his attitude gets right that he finally wakes up one day and Groundhog day is over and now he has a new life.

The adjustment that he made is what we need to make as well! At some point, you've got to get over what happened. You've got to get past what happened to you or what you did. You've got to change your attitude. You've got to realize that God still has a future for you. You're still breathing. You still have an opportunity to make a mark in this world. You have an opportunity to be a blessing to others. You have an opportunity for God to do something great in your life. You've got to go ahead and take advantage of that opportunity. Learn, grow and follow God's leading into the future he has for you!

# CHAPTER 13: GOD'S GOING TO DO A NEW THING!

If you start doing any research about second marriages, how hard it is to find a spouse when you're older or about how difficult it is to find a spouse when you already have kids, you're going to be tempted to be discouraged. The numbers don't look good. My favorite movie series of all time is Star Wars. One of my favorite lines is spoken by Han Solo. He says, "never tell me the odds!" Why? Because he believed he could always beat him, and he always did. And you know what? If you're a follower of Jesus, with God's help, you can beat them as well.

For with God nothing will be impossible. Luke 1:37 NKJV

These are the words of the angel that appeared to Mary and told her that she's going to have a baby even though she'd never been with a man. He then tells her that her family member, Elizabeth, who was much older and barren, was already pregnant. These are two impossible things that are happening right now in her life. Nothing is impossible when God gets involved!

I was recently on a trip to the Tulsa Dream Center. One of the guys there named AJ said something I never heard before (I told him I'd give him credit once so here it is!). When you see the word impossible, turn it around and realize God is saying, *I'm possible*. It may seem impossible but don't worry about it because He's possible.

God is able to do whatever he promised you. God has a Bae for you! No matter what your past is, God has somebody in mind for you. He's already written your love story.

> Now there was a wealthy & influential man in Bethlehem named Boaz, who was a relative of Naomi's husband, Elimelech. Ruth 2:1 NLT

I think a great example of this is what happened to Ruth. In the book of Ruth we read about a wealthy and kind man, named Boaz, who eventually notices Ruth. Ruth was a little bit older and a widow. Coming to this town was a big move in her life but she had ultimately decided that she was going to serve the God of the Bible and her mother-in-law. However there's no real natural hope for her marrying this kind of guy. He is established. He is important. He is wealthy. This is the kind of guy that can get any young virgin that he wants. Yet, this is the guy that God had in mind for Ruth and she lived happily ever after with that guy. Well, God did it for Ruth and God can do it for you. You only need one! And whether it's your Ruth or your Boaz, God has them waiting for you.

## Be Open to God doing a New Thing

> Do not remember the former things, Nor consider the things of old. Behold, I will do a new thing, Now it shall spring forth; Shall you not know it? I will even make a road in the wilderness, and rivers in the desert. Isaiah 43:18, 19 NKJV

God is telling you what to think about and what not to think about. He saying to not even recount what happened in the past. There does come a point where you kind of go, "Okay, I've thought about it. I've learned from it. Now it's time to forget about it." God is saying "Don't even remember what I did." Of course the things that he was talking about were good things, miracles that he had done. Yet he was saying not to even remember those things anymore because he was about to do something better!

It's going to be notable. You're going to know that He did this. It's going to be super natural. He mentions here creating a road right in the middle of the wilderness and creating rivers in the desert. God can do that, right?

There's one story in the Bible where the Bible talks about how there was an army stuck in the desert with no water. They were trying to go to war and yet were in danger of dying of thirst. God had prophet prophesy that there would be water there the next day. Sure enough, after they dug some ditches in faith, they woke up the next morning and water had found his way into the ditches in the middle of the desert!

> Then, being divinely warned in a dream that they should not return to Herod, they departed for their own country another way. Matthew 2:12 NKJV

Now God may do this in a way that you're not very familiar. This may not go down the way that you think it is going to go down. You need to be open to that. One thing that you can do, practically speaking, is kind of update your methods. The world has changed when it comes to dating. How people meet has changed. Sometimes we get caught up in the how, and we forget the what! What really matters is that you meet the person God has for you.

Some may say "I refuse to text!" or "I'm not going to FaceTime with anyone" or "There's no way I would ever join a Christian dating site!" But if God is prompting you to do it, then why wouldn't you do it? We've got these ideas in our head that get in the way of receiving God's best for our lives. "Well, you know, back in the day we used to..." Back in the day we had rotary phones too!"

There's a lot of things that change in this world. You can't get so caught up in what it used to be like, how things used to happen. Don't be so old fashioned that you miss out on what God wants to do in your life. What you need to do is you need to stay tuned into God about the who, the what, the when and how's of dating so that God can bring you in relationship with Bae.

My sister and her husband have a unique love story. She was in her mid-thirties and had never been married. She felt like God prompted her to join a Christian dating site. So she did. And the very first day she did, she came across this guy who lived in England. She lived in Dallas, Texas. They started talking and, of course, she's thinking that because he was in England there really wasn't much point in them pursuing a relationship with each other. However, over time, it became apparent that God may be doing something here. Eventually, they indeed got married. They have had an energetic little boy, my nephew, and they are very happy together.

She often preaches about what God is done in her life. She's got a great marriage and she's got a miracle baby (the doctor's had said she was unable to have children). What's wild is that all of this started because she joined a Christian dating site whenGod prompted her to do it!

God had a plan to bring them two together. He just did it in a way that was different. God has a plan for you, too. He has a plan for you to meet Bae. You need to be open to it. You need to be open to God's way of doing things. By the way, when you do meet the person that God has for you, you need to treat your new relationship, like a new relationship. Don't bring any of the old into this new thing that God is doing.

> The Spirit of the Lord God is upon Me, Because the Lord has anointed Me... To console those who mourn in Zion, To give them beauty for ashes, The oil of joy for mourning, The garment of praise for the spirit of heaviness; That they may be called trees of righteousness, The planting of the Lord, that He may be glorified. Isaiah 61:1, 3 NKJV

Jesus is anointed to give you beauty for ashes. In fact, if you were to study the word beauty there its talking about an embellishment, like a fancy head dress. It's talking about something that is not just functional, but beautiful. Jesus is saying that he can take what were ashes in your life, that house that was burned down and turn into something beautiful. The Message translation says it this way, *"I can give you bouquets of roses instead of ashes."*

Your life may have been burned down because of the choices of others or your own choices but I've got good news for you today. Jesus gives beauty for ashes. That's just what he does. That's part of his package. That's part of the salvation package. God is a God of restoration!

In Joel 2, it says that he's a God who will restore the years that have been eaten lost because of your negative choices. God is a God who specializes in restoring you. He specializes in causing you to not only get back to where you were, but taking you to even higher heights. God is a God who can take you from bitter to sweet. You can get to the place where you say, "man, I remember what I went through. I remember how bad it was, but now look at me, look at what God has done! Look at how sweet my life is!"

You can be like they were in Psalm 126! It will be like a dream!

You'll be laughing and singing and saying "I'm so happy because of what God did for me!" Your future with Bae is going to be just like that. It is bright.

So follow God's plan for you. Allow God to help you to recognize the facts about your situation, allow God to heal you, learn from your past relationships, ignore the stats and be ready for God to do a new thing. That's exactly what he's going to do, God's going to do a new thing in your life. And it's going to be a good thing. You're going to enjoy God's Bae for you.

# ABOUT THE AUTHOR

## Andre Butler

With an undeniable passion for equipping others to experience the future God has for them, Andre Butler is on a mission to share God's desire to prosper His people in every area of their lives, and His command for them to do their part in winning the world to Jesus. The Pastor of Faith Xperience Church (FX Church) in Downtown Detroit  and President of Andre Butler Ministries and Faith Xperience Films, he is a sought-after conference speaker and host known for his practical and relatable approach to preaching God's word.

A graduate of Rhema Bible Training Center, Pastor Andre also holds a bachelor's degree in Management from Kennesaw State University. He resides in Metro Detroit.

You can find his messages on Youtube and follow him on Tik Tok, Instagram, Clubhouse & Facebook. To book Pastor Andre connect with him on AndreButler.com.

# BOOKS BY THIS AUTHOR

**God's Future For You**

**Yxist: Find Your Y**

**Its Gonna Be Alright**

**You Can Win**

**Not In My House**

# FOLLOW PASTOR ANDRE

YouTube - Youtube.com/PastorAndreButler

Tik Tok - iamAndreButler

Instagram - Andre Butler

Twitter - Andre Butler

Facebook - Andre Butler

LinkedIn - Andre Butler

Faith Xperience Church - Myfaithx.com

Andre Butler Ministries - AndreButler.com

Match Made the Movie - MatchMadeMovie.com

Made in the USA
Columbia, SC
06 April 2021